ISRAEL

• AT COST •

A TRAVELLER'S GUIDE

LITTLE HILLS PRESS

© Photographs — Fay Smith
© Maps — Little Hills Press, 1990

Cover by Stuart Williams
Maps by Angela and Mark Butler
Typeset and printed in Singapore by Singapore National Printers Ltd.

© Little Hills Press, 1990
ISBN 1 86315 008 0

Little Hills Press Pty. Ltd.,
Tavistock House,
34 Bromham Road,
Bedford MK40 2QD
United Kingdom.

Regent House,
37–43 Alexander Street,
Crows Nest NSW 2065
Australia.

Distributed in USA and Canada by
The Talman Company, Inc
150 Fifth Avenue
New York NY 10011 USA

DISCLAIMER

Whilst all care has been taken by the publisher and author to
ensure that the information is accurate and up to date, the
publisher does not take responsibility for the information pub-
lished herein. The recommendations are those of the author and as
things get better or worse, places close and others open, some
elements in the book may be inaccurate when you get there. Please
write and tell us about it so we can update in subsequent editions.

COVER
The Lion's Gate, Old Jerusalem
Photograph by Fay Smith

CONTENTS

LIST OF MAPS

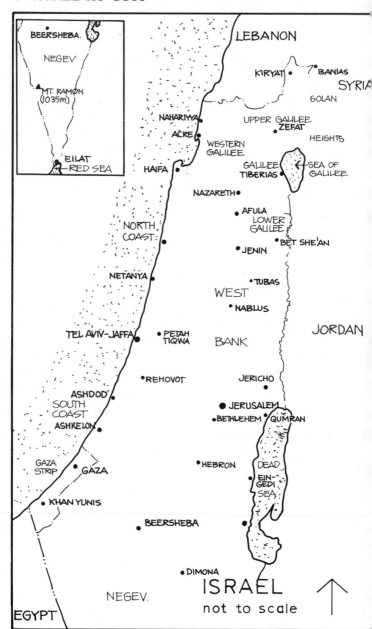

ISRAEL

Israel, the Holy Land, has great significance to Jews, Christians and Muslims. It was here that Solomon built his temple, Jesus Christ was born, lived and died, and Muhammad ascended to Heaven.

Israel has an area of 21,940km² (8,474 sq miles) and is bordered by Egypt to the south and west, Lebanon and Syria to the north and Jordan to the east. It is long and narrow, being 415km (260 miles) from north to south and 110km (70 miles) at its maximum width.

The northern and central part of Israel, where most of the population is concentrated, is divided into three distinct longitudinal strips; to the west, the coastal plain with the large cities of Tel Aviv and Haifa; to the east, the Jordan and Arava Valleys with the River Jordan linking the two inland seas, the mountain range that includes the hills of Galilee, Samaria and Judea with Jerusalem. In the north-east rise the Golan Heights and snow-capped Mt Hermon; and in the south stretch the deserts of the Negev and the Arava, which constitute a large proportion of the country, with Beersheva, the capital of Negev, and Elait on the Red Sea. Altitudes vary from the 1,208m (3,962 ft) of Mt Meron in Upper Galilee, to the −392m (−1,286 ft) of the Dead Sea.

Jerusalem is the capital and best-known city in Israel, but the largest city is Tel Aviv, which is situated on the Mediterranean coastline, and which has incorporated the city of Jaffa, said to be the oldest port in the world founded by a son of Noah, Japhet.

HISTORY

FROM ABRAHAM TO DAVID
The Old Testament of The Bible is the most authoritative account of Israel's ancient history. The book Genesis is thought to have been written c 1950-1445BC. Jerusalem is first mentioned as Salem, when Melchizedek, the king of Salem, gave bread and wine to Abraham (Gen.14:18–20). When God made his convenant with

Abraham, He gave to Abraham's descendants many lands including Canaan, which included the city of Salem.

Incidentally, it is thought that the unrest between Arabs and Jews stems from this period. Abraham had two sons, the eldest being Ishmael, whose mother was Hagar, a maid-servant. His second son was Isaac, whose mother was Sarah, Abraham's wife. Isaac, being a legitimate son, was Isaac's heir, although Ishmael was the eldest, and Sarah naturally enough wanted Ishmael cast out. God told Abraham to go along with Sarah, but not to worry because he would make Ishmael the beginning of a nation (Gen.21:9–13). Obviously Isaac became the father of the Jews, and Ishmael is said to have been the father of the Arabs.

For a few hundred years the Jews dwelt in Egypt, until Moses led them back to the Promised Land, parting the Red Sea on the way. He was not allowed to enter the 'land of milk and honey', but God at least allowed him to see it before he died on Mount Nebo in the land of Moab.

Then Joshua took the reins, crossed the Jordan, and destroyed Jericho. This is one of the few points on which Biblical students and archaeologists disagree. Excavations at the ancient site of Jericho have as yet failed to uncover anything resembling a wall from the period when Joshua and his army marched around the city blowing their trumpets (Joshua 6).

By about 1000BC the tribes of Israel had conquered the lands north and south of Jerusalem, and David became King of all Israel. He and his army camped before the city of Jerusalem, and the Jebusite inhabitants taunted him by placing the lame and blind on the city walls as a defence force (2 Sam.5:6–8). But one of his men had found the Gihon Spring from which the city drew its water, and a vertical shaft was built enabling the army to enter and overthrow the city. David was an outstanding leader, poet, musician, soldier and administrator and he enlarged the city of Jerusalem and brought it to new importance. He gathered materials for the Temple, but God did not allow him to build it as he had blood on his hands (1 Chron.22:7–8).

FIRST TEMPLE PERIOD
David's son, Solomon reigned from 971-931BC, and built the magnificent first Temple north of Mount Moriah (now the Dome

of the Rock), which had also been the site of the near-sacrifice of Isaac by Abraham (Gen.22:9–12). Solomon's wisdom has become legendary, especially his judgement of the argument between the two mothers over one live child (1 Kings 3:16–28), but he should also be remembered for the prosperity he brought to Israel, and the many fine buildings he caused to be erected. By the way, Solomon had 700 wives and 300 concubines (maybe he wasn't so wise after all!). One of his wives was the sister of the Pharoah of Egypt. There is one school of thought that the Queen of Sheba who visited Solomon was actually the Egyptian Queen, Hatshepsut, who had been married to Pharoah Thutmosis II, and reigned in her own right after his death. Her mortuary temple on the West Bank of the Nile in Luxor is reminiscent of descriptions of the Temple of Solomon.

After Solomon died the kingdom was divided into the Kingdom of Israel, comprising the northern ten tribes, with Jeroboam as king, and the Kingdom of Judah with the very weak Rehoboam, Solomon's son, as king. The two kingdoms were consantly at loggerheads. Jerusalem remained the capital of Judah, but was repeatedly invaded, most notably by Shishak (Thutmosis III) king of Egypt, who stripped the Temple of its wealth (2 Chron.12:9).

Around 865BC, Ahab, King of Israel, and Jehosophat, King of Judah, agreed on peace between the two kingdoms. Ahab's wife was the infamous Jezebel, who introduced the worship of the pagan god Baal, exerted a strong influence over Ahab, generally created havoc, and came to a very sticky end (2 Kings.9:30–37).

The period from 800 to 750BC was one of prosperity and expansion under Jeroboam II of Israel and Uzziah of Judah. But it was also a period of immorality, which was duly denounced by the prophets Hosea and Amos.

In 722BC the Kingdom of Israel was defeated by the Assyrians and most of its population exiled, bringing about the so-called Ten Lost Tribes of Israel. Meanwhile the Kingdom of Judah was absorbed by the Assyrian Empire. Then in 701BC Hezekiah, King of Judah, led a revolt against the Assyrians, bringing about a full-scale war. Hezekiah had brought the people back to their religion, and restored temple worship. He was also a brilliant engineer and had fortified the city of Jerusalem and built a completely new water system, enabling him to withstand the assault of

Sennacherib, the Assyrian king. Of course in all of this he was aided and influenced by Isaiah, the prophet (2 Chron.32:20).

However, in 697BC, the twelve-years-old Manasseh became King of Judah, and the people slipped back into their old pagan habits (2 Chron.33:1–9). He reigned for 55 years. Then came Josiah, the last great King of Judah, who once again insituted a religious reform, but was killed in 609BC at Megiddo, attempting to stem an Egyptian invasion. The prophet of doom in this case was Jeremiah, who also announced an approaching national catastrophe.

586BC saw the end of Judah. The city of Jerusalem was destroyed by Nebuchadnezzar, King of Babylon, and the people taken captive.

SECOND TEMPLE PERIOD

But nothing lasts for ever, particularly empires, and the Babylonians were defeated by the Persians in 539BC. In 537BC exiled Jews were allowed to return to their homeland. Zerubbabel arrived in Jerusalem in 536BC with 50,000 exiles to rebuild the city. The Second Temple was begun in 520BC and dedicated in 516BC. This was the beginning of what is known as the Second Temple Period.

Then it was the Persians' turn to suffer defeat in 333BC at the hands of Alexander the Great. Judea, as it was now known, came under Greek rule, as did all the surrounding countries. Alexander died 10 years later, and in the free-for-all that followed among his successors, Ptolemy from Egypt gained control of Judea.

The Second Temple Period was one of general upheaval and revolts, and disagreements among the Jews themselves about their religion. There were some religious groups who followed the established religion to the letter of the law, and others who modified it with parts of the religion of whichever country was in power. In 167BC three Maccabaean brothers, who started the Hasmonean dynasty, led a revolt against interference in the practice of their religion by the Seleucids, who were then in control. This led to an extension of Jewish dominance throughout the country. Then in 63BC, Pompey, the Roman general marched on the city of Jerusalem and took it for the Romans, beginning four centuries of Roman rule.

On to the scene now comes one of the great villians of history — Herod the Great. He was appointed King of the Jews by Mark Antony in 40BC, although he did not claim his throne until 37BC. On the plus side Herod rebuilt the city of Jerusalem and the Temple and also built forts at Massada, Caesarea, Herodion and other strongholds. But along the way he murdered his wife, his son, all the male children in Bethlehem who were two years and under in case any of them could be the Messiah (Matt.3:16), and anyone else who got in his way. He was also one of the greatest sycophants of all time, at least where the Romans were concerned, and definitely not of sound mind. He died around 4BC, and was buried 3km (4 miles) south-east of Bethlehem at the Herodium.

BIRTH OF CHRIST

Sometime around 5BC Jesus Christ was born in Bethlehem. The followers of Jesus believed him to be the Messiah. Many Jews were converted to the new religion of Christianity, while others refused to accept that Christ was the son of God, but thought him merely another prophet. The Jewish leaders, chief priests and pharisees could not come to terms with the fact that here was a man the people were willing to follow, and who could, they thought, easily set himself up as king, in other words, someone they had to dispose of. Anyway, the Jewish priests and the Roman officials got together, and we all know the end of that story. As a consequence, we have the world wide influence of Christian culture to the present day.

THE GREAT REVOLT

In 66AD the Great Revolt broke out, and the Jews drove the Romans out of their country and for a time were full of their own importance. Not for long though, for one year later the Romans took Galilee when the Jewish commander defected to the enemy. This commander was Josephus, or Flavius Josephus, who wrote a first hand (though biased) account in his book *The Jewish War*.

Then in 70AD the city of Jerusalem fell to the Roman general Titus after a siege of 134 days, as foretold by Christ (Luke 19:41–44). Titus destroyed the Temple and set fire to the city. The people were slaughtered, or taken into slavery, and the Great Revolt was at an end. Masada, the last stronghold, fell in 73AD, with its 960 defenders taking their own lives rather than surrendering.

The Emperor Hadrian decided to build a pagan city on the site of Jerusalem in 131AD. This led to a revolt led by Bar-Kochba, who scored some early successes. Then Bar-Kochba died in 135AD and the Romans, although suffering huge losses, suppressed the revolt, and destroyed what was left of Jerusalem. Hadrian then went ahead and built his city, called Aelia Capitolina, which was off-limits to Jews. He also changed the name of the country from Judea to Palaestina to try to get rid of the Jewish identity, outlawed the Jewish religion, and built a Temple of Jupiter on the Temple site. The Sanhedrin (highest court of justice and supreme council in ancient Jerusalem) was relocated in the Lower Galilee.

In 312AD Constantine the Great made Christianity the official religion of the Empire. His mother, Helena, a long-time convert went to the Holy Land in 326 and commenced restoration of some of the sacred sites. It was she who chose the site for the Church of the Holy Selpuchre, with which some now disagree.

In 351 there was another Jewish revolt against the Romans, this time the ruler Gallus, but it was mainly confined to the Galilee.

Julian the Apostate, Emperor from 361 to 363, tried to re-introduce the pagan cults in an effort to reduce Christianity. He was in favour of rebuilding the Temple in Jerusalem, but the project was held up by earthquake and fire — maybe divine intervention?

During the reign of Emperor Justinian (527–565), many important Churches were built or rebuilt, among them the Church of the Nativity in Bethlehem. Excavations throughout the country have uncovered a large number of synagogues from this period, showing that the Jewish religion was alive, if not too well.

Then came a Persian invasion in 614. The Byzantines defeated them in 628. However a more serious menace was rising to the south, in Arabia.

ISLAMIC INVASION

With the death of Muhammad in 632, the Arab Empire was headed by a Caliph, the religious, political and military leader. Among Islam's 'pillars of faith' is the tenet of Jihad, (Holy War) against any who oppose Islam. So within a hundred years of

Muhammad's death, the Arab empire stretched from Spain to India. They invaded Palestine in 636, and in 638 Jerusalem fell to the Caliph Omar. In 691 the Caliph Abd el-Malik built the Dome of the Rock in Jerusalem, near the site of the First Temple.

Israel then passed from one group of Muslims to another — in 775 the Abbasids, in 969 the Egyptians and in 1071, the Seljuk Turks.

THE CRUSADES

In 1099 the armies of the First Crusade reached the Holy Land, determined to wrest the Christian holy places from Muslim control. In a most un-Christian display, Jerusalem was taken and most of its inhabitants, both Jew and Muslim, slaughtered. In 1100 the Crusaders established the Latin Kingdom of Jerusalem with Baldwin I as its leader. By 1110 most of the coastal cities were in Crusader hands, making sure of the supply lines to Europe. In 1187 however, the Crusader armies were well and truly beaten by Saladin near the Sea of Galilee, and the Crusaders quit the country to regroup. The Third Crusade arrived in 1191, led by Richard the Lionheart of England and Philip II of France, but although this army managed to capture the coastal towns from Tyre to Jaffa, it never regained the size of the Latin Kingdom of Jerusalem of 1100. Akko (Acre) was made the royal capital.

1291 saw the end of the Crusader Kingdom when it was defeated by the Mameluke Sultan Baybars, and the Muslims were back in control. There then existed a period of comparative peace for about 250 years.

RETURN OF ISLAM

In the early 16th century, the Ottoman Turks extended their power throughout the Middle East, with Jerusalem falling to them in 1516. Suleiman the Magnificent (1520–1566) commenced many buildings in Jerusalem, and rebuilt the walls and gates of the city which are standing to this day. When Suleiman died the great Ottoman Empire went into a decline, and Jerusalem with it.

The next would-be invader was Napoleon Bonaparte in 1799, but he didn't get any further than Akko. Then Egyptians under Muhammed Ali and Ibrahim Pasha took control of Israel. They were thrown out in 1840 with the help of European nations which wanted diplomatic, religious and economic concessions in Israel.

In 1869, the opening of the Suez Canal brought about increased competition between the European powers for control of the region. During World War I, in November 1917, Jerusalem was taken by the British leader, General Allenby, thereby ending the Ottoman Empire.

BRITISH MANDATE

The League of Nations granted Great Britain a 'mandate' to govern Palestine in 1920, with Sir Herbert Samuel as the first high commissioner. Although Britain, in the Balfour Declaration, had declared she would do her best to help the establishment in Palestine of a national home for the Jewish people, she was actually playing both sides against the middle, as Britain was also keen to encourage an Arab rebellion against the Turks.

Jordan, which had originally been part of the British mandate, became a separate kingdom in 1923, and Arab attacks on the Jews accelerated in 1929. In spite of this continuing threat, Jewish immigration to Palestine increased until a British Parliamentary Commission to report on rioting recommended that restrictions be placed on Jewish immigration, and that they be prohibited from buying Arab land.

With the rise of Hitler's regime in Germany and the threat of war, Britain wanted to appease the Arabs, afraid that they would support the Germans, so greater restrictions were placed on Jewish immigration. As many Jews wanted to flee Europe, the result was illegal immigration in often unseaworthy ships which the British intercepted and sometimes sank. It was worth the risk for the Jews, because their future in Europe was bleak. Jewish terrorist groups were formed.

With the outbreak of World War II in 1939, local Jews threw themselves behind the Allied cause, and put their personal fight with Britain aside for a time. When the war ended, and the details of the Holocaust became clear, the Jews were more determined than ever to have their own state, and the Arabs just as determined to keep them out of Palestine. There were acts of terrorism and atrocities committed by both sides, with Jews, Arabs and British being killed and tortured.

On May 14, 1948 the British mandate ended, their troops withdrew, and the State of Israel was proclaimed. That night the

Eyptian air force bombed Tel Aviv, and the Arab invasion started
the next day.

INDEPENDENCE

Amazingly, the Jews won this War of Independence, and
expanded their boundaries beyond those granted by the United
Nations, but the Jordanians held the Old City of Jerusalem. The
result did nothing to restore peace, though, and raiding parties
from both sides continued to create havoc.

In 1956, Britain and France launched the Suez campaign against
Egypt to stop Nasser, the new Egyptian leader, from taking
control of the Suez Canal. Israel was persuaded to join in their
attempt, and indeed played its part by invading Egypt across the
Sinai, but the British and French retreated because of criticism
from the United States, the United Nations and the Soviet Union.
Israel was forced to withdraw too, but only after a UN Security
Force had been stationed in the Sinai.

Nassar ordered the UN force out of the Sinai in 1967, and
replaced them with his own troops, and King Hussein of Jordan
placed his army under Egyptian command, thereby massing the
Arabs for a Holy War against the Jews.

The war, known as The Six Day War, lasted from June 5 to June
10, and the Israelis were again victorious. Their territory now
included the whole of the Sinai to the Suez Canal, the entire West
Bank (including the Old City of Jerusalem, except the Temple site)
and the Golan Heights on the Syrian border.

The result of this victory brought a feeling of complacency and
invincibility to the Israelis, so it was a complete shock to them
when in October 1973, on Yom Kippur, the holiest day of the
Jewish calendar, the Egyptian and Syrian armies attacked Israel.
The Israelis drove them back, with enormous loss of life, but their
confidence was shattered. The successful raid on Entebbe airport
in Uganda in 1976, to rescue a hijacked aircraft, relieved their
doubts in this regard to some extent.

After he took office in 1977, Israeli Prime Minister Menachem
Begin quietly campaigned for a meeting with President Sadat of
Egypt. Sadat went to Jerusalem and the pair met at Camp David in

the US at a meeting organised by President Jimmy Carter. The treaty between Egypt and Israel in March, 1979, ended 30 years of hostility between them, and Israel withdrew from the Sinai.

So now there is peace with Egypt, but Israel still has its problems with other Arab nations, notably Syria and Iraq, and, of course, there is always the constant presence of the PLO.

CLIMATE

Israel has a Mediterranean climate, with pleasant springs and autumns. Winters in the north can be quite cool. Rain is widespread in winter only, particularly in Jerusalem. Snow is rare, but it does fall in the mountains.

Average temperatures in Jerusalem range from 11C (53F) in January to 30C (86F) in August. In Tel Aviv, the hottest months are July/August with an average of 30C (86F), and the coldest is January with 18C (65F). Eilat, on the Red Sea, averages 40C (103F) in July/August, and 21C (70F) in January.

POPULATION

Israel has a population of around 4 million, made up of 3,365,000 Jews, 640,000 Moslems and 80,000 Christians. There are also around 50,000 Druze, a religious sect which is an offshoot of Islam.

The Jews are divided into two main groups — the Ashkenazim, who come from central Europe, and the Sephardim, who are descendants of Jews exiled from Spain in 1492 at the time of the Inquisition.

LANGUAGE

Hebrew, the revived language of the Bible, and Arabic are the official languages of Israel. However, as the result of the immigration of peoples from all over the world, many languages are spoken, including English, French, Polish and Hungarian.

RELIGION

As mentioned above, the majority of Israelis are Jewish, and their Shabat (sabbath) begins at sunset on Friday and ends at sunset on

Saturday. During the Shabat religious Jews do no work, consequently there is virtually no public transport, and banks, post offices, shops and restaurants are closed. In actual fact things start to ease off about lunchtime on Friday.

The Arab areas are of course not affected by the Shabat, their sabbath begins at sundown on Thursday, but most of them work on Friday until noon.

HOLIDAYS

Visitors can be affected by Jewish religious and public holidays, either by the closure of restaurants, movie-theatres, the shutting down of the public transport system, or simply by the increase in accommodation rates. It is wise to check with your travel agent before you leave, as most of the holidays are controlled by the sun, the moon, or a combination of both.

Here is a very general guide:

January–February: *Tu b'Shevat*, Israeli Arbor Day, is celebrated, naturally enough, with the planting of trees.

March: *Purim*, Feast of Lots, commemorating a time when Queen Esther saved her people in Persia (5th century BC). There are street parades, with people in fancy dress.

April: *Pesach*, Passover, celebrates the exodus of the Israelites from Egypt. The first night of the holiday there is a seder, a family meal and service, and for the rest of the week most Jews eat only unleavened bread. Some restaurants have special seders for tourists, and the tourist information office would have details. The first and last days of this holiday are like the Shabat, so many places are closed.

May: *Israel Independence Day*.

May–June: *Shavuot*, Pentecost, is the harvest celebration. *Lag b'Omer*, ending 33 days of mourning, is the chief celebration of the Hasidim, who leave Jerusalem at this time to visit the Meron tomb of Rabbi Shimon Bar Yochai in Galilee. They sing, dance and light bonfires.

July–August: *Tisha b'Av* is a fast day and remembers the destruction of the First and Second Temples. All places of entertainment are closed.

September–October: *Rosh Hashannah*, Jewish New Year, is the start of the High Holy Days. This is a two-day religious festival, a time for contemplation and prayer.

Yom Kippur, the Day of Atonement, is held a week after Rosh Hashannah, and is the most solemn of Jewish holidays. It is a fast day, but hotel dining rooms still serve guests. For the Jews, most of the day is spent in the synagogues, and all public facilities are closed, including television and radio stations.

Sukkoth, is held five days after Yom Kippur, and is a seven-day period recalling how Moses and the Children of Israel dwelt in 'booths' when they left Egypt to wander in the desert. Some families have meals and services in specially built huts in gardens or on balconies. This is also a harvest festival (Feast of the Tabernacles). The last day, *Simchat Torah*, marks the end of the reading of the Five Books of Moses.

December: *Hanukkah* commemorates the victory of the Maccabees over Syrian-Greeks who outlawed Jewish religious practices in 164BC. The menorah, the symbol of this holiday, is lit nightly for the eight nights of the festival.

Christmas and Easter are celebrated by the Christian population with special reverence. The festivities for Christmas begin at Bethlehem on December 24 with a procession at noon, and in the evening choirs from all over the world sing in Manger Square. Midnight mass is shown, for those that can't get into the church, on a giant TV screen in the square. The Greek Orthodox ceremonies take place on January 6, and the Armenian on January 17.

On Palm Sunday there are processions from the Mount of Olives which continue throughout Holy Week, ending with the Procession of the Cross along the Via Dolorosa on Good Friday. Hundreds of pilgrims crowd into the Church of the Holy Sepulchre on Holy Saturday for the Ceremony of the Holy Fire, and several Protestant sunrise services are held in Jerusalem on Easter Sunday.

The most religious time for the Muslims is the month of Ramadan (in June), when the followers fast from sunrise to sunset. The completion of the fast is the three-day festival, Id el-Fitr.

ENTRY REGULATIONS

Visitors to Israel require a passport which is valid for a minimum of six months from the date of departure from Israel. Nationals of Australia, Canada, New Zealand, United Kingdom and United States do not require a Visa to visit Israel.

Health Regulations
Certificates of vaccination are not required, but health authorities advise protection against Typhoid and Polio. Rabies is present, and those at high risk should seek medical advice before leaving home.

Mains water is normally chlorinated, and although relatively safe, may cause mild stomach upsets. Bottle water is recommended and is widely available.

Customs Allowance
The following goods may be imported into Israel free of customs duty.

250 cigarettes or 250 grams tobacco products
1 litre of spirits
2 litres of wine
0.25 litre of eau de cologne or perfume
Gifts up to US$125.

Please note that anyone visiting Israel with a video camera has to pay a deposit before the equipment can be taken into the country. Please check with the Israel Embassy in your home country as to the amount and method of payment.

NOTE: If you are continuing on from your tour of Israel to Jordan, Syria, the Sudan, or other Arab nations, except Egypt, it is imperative that you ask the Israeli officials at the border not to stamp your passport. They will usually oblige and stamp a removable piece of paper. You will be refused entry to these Arab nations, and to some in Africa, if you have an Israeli stamp in your passport.

EXIT REGULATIONS

If you are leaving Israel by air, the departure tax is included in your airline ticket. If by bus, there is a departure tax, payable at the border, of US$19.00 or 38NIS.

A maximum of the equivalent of US$50 may be converted on leaving the country. Anything in excess of this must be supported by a receipt from the original exchange transaction. In reality, you are better to get rid of your Shekels before you leave.

EMBASSIES

Australia	:	Australian Embassy, Beit Europa, 37 Shaul Hamelech Boulevarde, Tel Aviv 64928, ph 250 451.
Canada	:	Canadian Embassy, 220 Rehov Hayarkon, Tel Aviv, 63405, ph 228 122/6.
New Zealand	:	No resident representative. Refer to The Netherlands (NZ Embassy, Mauritskade 25, The Hague 2514HD, ph 31-70-469 324).
U.K.	:	Consulate-General, 198 Hayarkon Street, Tel Aviv, 63405, ph 242 105/6.
U.S.	:	US Ambassador, 71 Hayarkon Street, Tel Aviv, ph 654 338.

MONEY

The unit of currency is the New Israeli Shekel (NIS), which equals 100 Argorot. Notes are in demoninations of 5, 10, 50 and 100 new shekels, and coins in 1 and 5 new argorot, half and 1 new shekel. Please note that 1 new shekel (which was introduced in 1986) equals 1000 old shekels.

Approximate exchange rates are:—
A$ = 1.50NIS
Can$ = 1.77NIS
NZ$ = 1.17NIS
UK£   = 3.30NIS
US$ = 2.00NIS

While travellers cheques are definitely the safest way of carrying money overseas, it is advisable to carry some American dollars in cash. When it is not possible to exchange the cheques, due to lack of facilities, you will find that everyone will accept the greenback, even the small souvenir shops.

Accommodation rates are in US Dollars, as payment in a foreign currency does not attract VAT.

Banking Hours
In the major cities and towns the banking hours are:
   Sun, Tues, Thurs — 8.30am–12.30pm and 4–5.30pm.
   Mon, Wed — 8.30am–12.30pm only.
   Fri (or eve of holy day) — 8.30am–12 noon.
   In East Jerusalem, they are slightly different:
   Mon–Thurs — 8.30am–2.30pm.
   Fri (or eve of Jewish holy day) — 8.30am–12.30pm.

COMMUNICATIONS

Full IDD services are available, and the country code is 972. Ordinary telex facilities are available to guests in most deluxe hotels in Jerusalem and Tel Aviv. Public telex booths are at 23 Rehov Yaffo, Jerusalem and 7 Rehov Mikve Yisrael, Tel Aviv.

Post Office Hours
Sun–Thurs — 8.30am–1pm
Fri — 8.30am–12.30pm.

Most 4- and 5-star hotels have facsimile services.

Newspapers are printed in many languages, with the English language paper being the *Jerusalem Post*, on Sundays to Friday.

MISCELLANEOUS

Local time is GMT + 2 hours, and there is no daylight saving in Israel.

Electrical current is 220 volts AC.

Israel uses the metric system for weights and measures.

Clothing
Although you may be intending to visit Israel in the hotter months, you are advised to remember that entrance to holy sites (which sometimes can mean just a collection of old rocks and ruins) depends on how you are dressed. No shorts are allowed, knees must be covered. The same goes for shoulders, your gear must have sleeves. Men also have to wear hats when visiting a synagogue, and ladies when visiting sacred sites, but this is no problem, as a hat in Israel is a necessary item — you have to take your own shade to a lot of the sites.

Women should keep in mind that they are in a country far removed from our western culture, and remember to dress accordingly if they don't want to attract unwelcome attention.

It is also recommended that you pack a torch (flashlight), because some of the underground sites have no lighting.

It is advisable to buy a water bottle, or canteen, before you leave home. The bottled water, which is called 'mineral water' but tastes like pure water, comes with a seal, which is not much good once the bottle has been opened. Always carry water with you, and make sure you drink a couple of litres a day to prevent dehydration.

Israel has excellent medical facilities. Health centres are marked by the red Star of David on a white background. We recommend you take out medical insurance.

Tipping was once scorned as demeaning, but Israelis have caught up with the rest of the world, and a tip is appreciated. Usually about 10 to 15% should suffice. If a taxi driver is not using his meter, you can be sure he has already added his tip to the agreed price.

When reading about Israel, or when travelling around it, you will come across the word 'tel'. When an ancient civilisation built a city there was usually a good reason for its location, such as the proximity of water or its defensive possibilities. Naturally enough the next civilisation that came along, maybe hundreds of years later, chose the same site, and simply built on top of the ruins of the previous one. As this kept happening the level of ground became higher, virtually forming a man-made mountain, or a 'tel'. Some that you visit will already have been excavated and evidence of the different inhabitants uncovered, but there are so many all over the country that some just appear to be plateaux in the middle of flat open ground.

The noticeboards at the various archaeological sites will have information about the history of the area, and after some of the dates there will appear the letters BCE. This stands for 'Before the Common Era', and means exactly the same as BC, but being a Jewish country, Israel does not date anything before or after Christ.

There seems to be a shortage of toilet tissue and paper towels in Israel, so it is best to carry tissues and moist toilettes. Outside of the hotels and restaurants, the best toilets are found in the national parks and nature reserves. Don't wait until you find a service station, you could be horribly disappointed at the standard of cleanliness.

The spelling of Israeli towns and sights varies from map to map, and can be confusing to the visitor. The reason is simply that the Hebrew and Arabic alphabets are not the same as the English alphabet, making translation difficult. The best way to get around the situation is: if the place *sounds* like the one you are looking for, although it is spelt differently, it probably is the right one.

The National Parks Authority has a 14-day ticket for 17.60 NIS which allows entry to 37 sites, and is very good value. You can pick it up at their office at 4 Rav Alluf M. Makleff Street, HaKirya, Tel Aviv, ph 25 22 81, or at any of the major sites.

When you tell your friends that you are going to Israel, someone is bound to say, "Aren't you frightened you'll get mixed up in all the fighting?" Don't let them put you off. Israel is a strongly defended country, and it is unlikely that an invasion will occur. In any case, tourists would not be allowed in any part of the country where there might be trouble.

Of course, you will see quite a number of armed soldiers, but remember that all Israelis (except religious students) must enter the army for a period of three years at the age of 18, and then do 30 days service every year up to the age of 55. Some that you see will be on leave, but they carry their weapons at all times. It is strange, though, to see a group of armed soldiers waiting at the bus stop, but you get used to it. By the way, when it comes to hitchhiking, by law soldiers have priority over private citizens (or visitors).

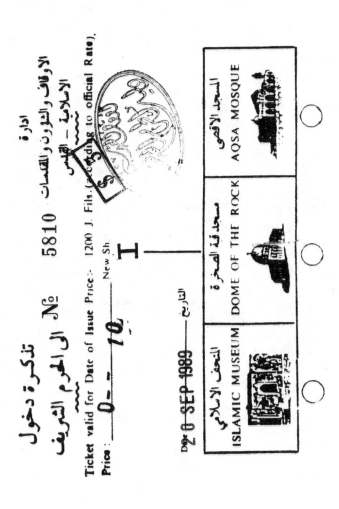

ادارة
الاوقاف والشؤون والمقدسات
الاسلامية — القدس

الارشاد والتوزن والقمامات
الاسلامية — القدس

تذكرة دخول
الى الحرم الشريف   № 5810

Ticket valid for Date of Issue Price:- 1200 J. Fils. (according to official Rate).

Price : ___ 0 ـــ 10 ___ New Sh.

التاريخ ___ Date 0 SEP 1989

التحف الاسلامي	سجد قبة الصخرة	المسجد الاقصى
ISLAMIC MUSEUM	DOME OF THE ROCK	AQSA MOSQUE

TRAVEL INFORMATION

HOW TO GET THERE

By Air

El Al Airlines is the national carrier and has flights to Tel Aviv from:

    Boston — once a week
    Chicago — once a week
    Los Angeles — twice a week
    New York — 3 times a week
    Montreal — twice a week
    Toronto — twice a week
    London — daily except Friday.

British Airways has flights to Tel Aviv from London — daily except Friday.

Canadian Airlines has flights to Tel Aviv from:

    Montreal — daily except Tuesday
    Toronto — daily except Tuesday
    Calgary — 5 times a week
    Edmonton — 5 times a week

Pan Am has flights to Tel Aviv from:

    Boston — daily
    Chicago — daily
    Los Angeles — daily
    New York — daily

Passengers from Australia and New Zealand cannot take a direct flight to Tel Aviv, but they do have a few alternatives.

For example, flying Olympic Air or Singapore Airlines to Athens, Greece, then El Al to Tel Aviv.

OR Qantas or Philippine Airlines to Manila in the Philippines, then Egypt Air via Cairo.

It is best to check current timetables with your travel agent, as some of these flights involve long transit stops, and you may have limited time. If it is necessary for a stop of several hours, check to see what facilities are available in the transit airport, or if you will be allowed out of the airport. In Athens, for example, Olympic Air arranges a day-use hotel room free of charge, which is a welcome relief after the long flight from down under.

Israel's international airport is Ben Gurion International at Lod about 20km (12 miles) out of Tel Aviv.

In front of the airport is the stop for the shuttle bus to Tel Aviv, which leaves every hour on the hour to the Central Railway Station in the northern part of the city, and then loops past all the major hotels.

The El Al airline bus to the company terminal in Tel Aviv departs after every El Al arrival.

The local Egged buses also leave from the airport for Tel Aviv every 15 minutes from 5am to 11.10pm; for Jerusalem approximately every 20 minutes from 7.15am to 6pm; for Haifa approximately every 20 minutes from 7am to 6pm.

By Sea

The principal ports for international passengers are Haifa and Ashdod.

Car ferries travel to Haifa from Venice, Piraeus (Athens), Iraklion (Crete), Rhodes and Limassol (Cyprus).

Stability Line, whose office is in Piraeus (11 Sahtouri Street, ph 414 3312) have an agent in Haifa — Mano Passenger Lines, 39–41 Ha-Meginim Avenue, ph 04-531 631. Their ferry the *Vergina* makes the trip Piraeus-Iraklion-Limassol-Haifa once a week from April to December.

Sol Lines have two ferries, the *Sol Phryne*, which sails Piraeus-Rhodes-Limassol-Haifa once a week, and the *Sol Olympia*, which sails Venice-Haifa every ten days. The latter is an extremely slow trip, and rather expensive.

Sol Lines' office in Athens is at Filellinon 4, ph 451 7709, in Rhodes at 11 Amerikis Street, ph 22 460, in Limassol at 1 Irene Street, ph 57 000. They are also represented by Mano Passenger Lines in Haifa.

Prudential Lines and Lykes Lines have cargo/passengers services from New York and Galveston in the United States to Haifa and Ashdod.

The Grimald/Siosa Lines have a service from Alexandria to Ashdod.

By Road

There is a bus service between Egypt and Israel which is operated jointly by Nizza Tours Israel, and Traveco Egypt. The trip takes about 7 hours, not including the time spent at the two borders, which could be anything from 2 to 4 hours. There are two stops for refreshments, one in Israel at a service station cum supermarket cum restaurant, and one in Egypt near the Suez Canal. The bus is air-conditioned, but the trip is extremely tedious, as there is not much to look at except sand.

Pick-up points for the trip are:

Jerusalem — Central Bus Station, departing 6.45am.

Tel Aviv — Atarim Square, Hayarkon Street, departing 7.30am.

Cairo — Cairo Sheraton Hotel, departing 4.30am.

Arrangements can be made for pick-up at different hotels, depending on the number of passengers involved.

Luggage is inspected at both borders, and there is a E£13 departure tax from Egypt. The time spent at the border stations is extremely frustrating, as there doesn't seem to be any reason for the delay.

Allenby Bridge, near Jericho, is the crossing-point between Israel and Jordan. Tourists may cross from Jordan to Israel and back again to Jordan, or from Israel to Jordan, but not back again to Israel. The visa requirements are the same as at any other port of entry into Israel. Private vehicles may not cross the bridge, and all cameras must be empty of film.

ACCOMMODATION

Israel offers a wide range of accommodation from 5-star hotels to simple guest houses.

There are hundreds of hotels listed by the Ministry of Tourism, and they vary from small to the most luxurious, with prices ranging according to grade and season. It is wise to book well in advance for the April — October period, and for religious holidays. We have listed hotels in the sections on the various towns.

On the Mediterranean Sea and the Red Sea Gulf, there are holiday villages which have cabin or bungalow accommodation, but they are usually only open between April and October.

KIBBUTZIM

Some of the kibbutzim located in scenic parts of the country have guesthouses which offer 3 to 4-star accommodation. Most of them have swimming pools, and all have excellent dining rooms. Information on these can be obtained from Kibbutz Rest and Guesthouses, PO Box 1139, Tel Aviv, or the following can be contacted direct:

Ayyelet haShahar — Upper Galilee — ph (06) 937 364.
Bet Hava — Shave Ziyyon — ph (04) 922 391.
Bet Oren — Mt Carmel — ph (04) 222 111.
Bet Yesha — Giv'at Brenner — ph (054) 50076.
Ein-Gedi — Dead Sea — ph (057) 90874.
Ein Gev — Lake Tiberias — (06) 751 167.
Gesher haSiw — Western Galilee — (04) 927 711.
Hafez Hayyim — Gedera — ph (055) 92 681.
HaGosherim — Upper Galilee — ph (06) 940 138.
Hof Dor — Carmel Coast — ph (06) 399 533.
Kayit veShayit — Caesarea — (06) 361 161.
Kefar Blum — Upper Galilee — (06) 940 468.
Kefar Gil'adi — Upper Galilee — (06) 741 414.
Lavi — Lower Galilee — (06) 721 477.
Ma'ale haHamisha — Judean Hills — (02) 539 591.
Nir 'Ezyon — Mt Carmel — (04) 942 542.
Nof Ginossar — Lake Tiberias — (06) 792 161.
Qiryat 'Anavim — Judean Hills — (02) 539 691.
Shefayyim — near Tel Aviv — (052) 70 171.
Shoresh — Judean Hills — (02) 538 171.

CHRISTIAN HOSPICES

The Tourist Office has information on the 30 or so Christian Hospices scattered throughout the country. The Hospices give preference to groups of pilgrims, but will take individuals if space allows. They have basic facilities.

CAMPING GROUNDS

Each region of the country has its share of camping grounds, with good facilities and clean bathroom/toilet areas. They usually have tents and cabins for hire, as well as all other necessary equipment. There is usually a swimming pool, or a place for swimming nearby. Here are a few you could contact direct.

Akhziv, Mobile Post Galil Ma'aravi — ph (04) 921 792.
Ashqelon, PO Box 5052 — ph (05) 36 777.
Bet Zayit, Mobile Post Hare Yehuda — ph (02) 537 717.
Bitan Aharon, Bitan Aharon 40294 — ph (053) 22 186.
Dor, Mobile Post Hof HaKarmel — ph (06) 399 018.
Elait, Sun Bay PO Box 96 — ph (059) 73105.
Ein-Gedi, Mobile Post Sedom — ph (057) 84 342.
En Gev, Mobile Post En Gev — ph (06) 758 027.
En Hemed, Bet Neqofa, Hare Yehuda — ph (02) 539 190.
HaOn, Mobile Post 'Emeq haYarden — ph (06) 757 555.
Harod, Mobile Post Gilbo'a — ph (06) 581 660.
Kefar Hittim, Mobile Post Galil Tahton — ph (06) 795 921.
Lehman, Mobile Post Galil Ma'aravi — ph (04) 926 206.
Ma'agan, Mobile Post 'Emeq haYarden — ph (06) 751 360.
Mevo Betar, Mobile Post Ha'Ela — ph (02) 912 474.
Newe Yam, Mobile Post Hof haKarmel — ph (04) 942 240.
Ramat Rahel, PO Box 98, Jerusalem — ph (02) 715 712.
Tal, Post Qiryat Shemona — ph (06) 940 400.
Yam haMelah (Newe Zohar), Post Sedom — ph (057) 84 306.
Yotvata (Ye'elim), Mobile Post Elot — ph (059) 74 362.

YOUTH HOSTELS

IYHA, PO Box 1075 (3 Dorot Rishonim), Jerusalem, ph (02) 222 073, have details of all the youth hostels in Israel. The hostels are either dormitory-style, family bungalows, or huts, and here is a list.

Akko, PO Box 1090 — ph (04) 911 982.
Arad "Bet Blau-Weiss", PO Box 34 — ph (057) 97 150.
Bar Giyyora, Mobile Post Mate Yehuda — ph (02) 911 073.
Be'er Sheva "Bet Yaziv", PO Box 7 — ph (057) 77 444.
Bet Me'ir "Ramot Shapira", PO Box 7216, Jerusalem — ph (02) 913 219.
Elait, PO Box 152 — ph (059) 72 358.
Ein-Gedi "Bet Sara", Mobile Post Yam haMelah — ph (057) 90 871.
Haifa "Karmel", Mobile Post Hof haKarmel — ph (04) 531 944.
Jerusalem
    "Bet Bernstein", 1 Keren haYesod Street — ph (02) 228 286.

"En Kerem", PO Box 17013 — ph (02) 416 282.

"Louid Waterman-Wise", Bayit veGan — ph (02) 423 366.

"Moreshet haYahadut", Jewish Quarter PO Box 7880 — ph (02) 288 611.

"Ya'ar Yerushalayim", PO Box 3353 — ph (02) 416 060.

Kare Deshe, "Yoram", Mobile Post Korazim — ph (06) 720 601.

Kefar Ezyon, Mobile Post Har Hevron — ph (02) 742 477.

Kefar Vitkin, Emeq Hefer — ph (053) 96 032.

Ma'yan Harod "Hankin", Mobile Post Gilbo'a — ph (06) 581 660.

Masada "Y.H. Taylor", Mobile Post Yam haMelah — ph (057) 84 349.

Mizpe Ramon "Bet No'am", PO Box 2 — ph (057) 88 443.

Poriyya "Taiber", PO Box 32, Teverya — ph (06) 750 050.

Petah Tiqwa, Yad leBanim, Yahalom Street — ph (03) 926 666.

Qiryat 'Anavim, "HaEzrahi" — ph (02) 539 770.

Qiryat Tiv'on, 12 Alexander Zeid Street — ph (04) 931 482.

Ramat haGolan "Hispin", Mobile Post Ramat haGolan — ph (06) 763 305.

Ramat Yohanan, Post Kef. haMaccabi — ph (04) 442 976.

Rosh Pinna, "Hoveve haTeva" — ph (06) 737 086.

Sullam Zor, "Yad laYad", Mobile Post Galil Ma'aravi — ph (04) 921 343.

Tel Aviv, PO Box 22078 — ph (03) 455 042.

Tel Hay, Mobile Post Galil 'Elyon — ph (06) 740 043.

Tiberias, PO Box 81 — ph (06) 721 775.

Zefat, PO Box 1139 — ph (06) 931 086.

APARTMENTS

Apartments and rooms are plentiful, and the following will be helpful:

Jerusalem

Anglo-Saxon Real Estate Agency, 2 Rehov Hassoreg, (PO Box 7046) ph (02) 221 161.

Bier Tuvya Real Estate Agency, 2 Rehov Keren Kayenet, ph (02) 639 784.

Carmi Ora Real Estate Agency, 8 Rehov Beit Hama'alot, ph (02) 233 030.

Dahaf, 43 Rehov Yafo, ph (02) 226 335.

Homtel Israel, 76 Rehov Haneerim, ph (02) 246 880.

Kaitanit, 18 Rehov Hahistadrut (PO Box 7373), ph (02) 234 945.

Rent-a-Room, c/- Patra, 52 Rehov Yafo, ph (02) 234 048.

Sheal-Baruch Malin Ltd, 7 Rehov Hillel, ph (02) 226 919.

Tel Aviv

Anglo-Saxon Real Estate Agency, 167 Rehov Hayarkon (PO Box 3036), ph (03) 286 181.

Homtel Israel, 33 Rehov Dizengoff, ph (03) 289 503.

Paradise, 43 Rehov Ben Yehuda, ph (03) 240 902.

Rent-a-Room, c/- Patra, 13 Rehov Nahalat Binyamin, ph (03) 623 415.

Haifa

Moshe Horowitz, Broker, 7 Rehov Nordau, Mt Carmel, ph (04) 665 938.

Richman and Richman Ltd, 5 Derech Hayman, ph (04) 84 444.

Shimon Wimmer, 2 Rehov Elhannan, Mt Carmel, ph (04) 85 250.

Netanya

Richman and Richman Ltd, 3 Rehov Sha'ar Hagai, ph (053) 39 954.

LOCAL TRANSPORT

Air

Israel's domestic airline is Arkia, and has the following scheduled flights:

From Jerusalem to Tel Aviv, Haifa, Rosh Pinna, Elait.

From Tel Aviv to Jerusalem, Rosh Pinna, Elait.

From Haifa to Jerusalem, Tel Aviv, Elait.

From Elait to Jerusalem, Tel Aviv, Haifa.

Arkia's main office is at Sde Dov, Tel Aviv's domestic airport, ph 03-413 222.

Bus

There are two main bus companies in Israel, Egged and Dan. Egged has services in nearly every city and town in the country, and intercity services, while Dan operates in Tel Aviv. Some of the buses are airconditioned, some are not.

The services start at 5.30am till late evening, Sunday to Thursday. On Friday and the eve of Jewish holidays, the service ends at 4pm, although the West Bank, East Jerusalem and Haifa have some buses on Friday evening and Saturday.

There is an information booth in the bus station of every town and city which has details of timetables and fares, or you can telephone the following — Tel Aviv 03-432 414, Jerusalem 02-528 231, Haifa 04-535 276, Eilat 059-75 161.

A fare of 1.00NIS will cover any route around cities. Buses between Jerusalem and Tel Aviv cost 4.80 NIS, with direct buses from Jerusalem to the airport costing 4.50 NIS.

Egged Tours also offer regular tours, from half-day to a week, to sites around the country, accompanied by experienced guides. Their office is at 15 Frishman Street, Tel Aviv, ph 03-244177.

Train
Israel Railways have a service from Nahariya to Beersheva and Dimona in the south, via Haifa, Tel Aviv and major towns of the north coast, and one from Haifa to Jerusalem, passing through the Judean wilderness. The route from Tel Aviv to Jerusalem is much slower than by road, but is very scenic.

As with the buses, trains do not operate during the Sabbath. Travel by train is slightly cheaper than by bus.

Taxi
All taxis in Israel are required to have a meter, but you usually have to insist that the driver turns it on.

Sheruts are shared taxis taking up to seven people per cab. Some operate seven days a week from stations or taxi stands in each city. Make sure you agree on the price before entering the sherut, as they do not have meters.

Most trips, intercity and intracity, have set fares, and the Tourist Office will have details.

Car
All the major car rental companies are represented in Israel, and will arrange for cars to be picked up at the airport.

Traffic drives on the right hand side of the road, and traffic signs are similar to those in Europe. An International driving licence is preferred, but some companies will accept licences of other countries who have diplomatic relations with Israel, providing the licence is in English or French.

The roads are quite good, but the local drivers are not so good, therefore it pays to drive very carefully in the cities. There are plenty of service stations, but most of them are closed on Saturday and Jewish holidays.

The following table gives some idea of the distances involved in touring Israel.

Distances from Jerusalem to —
— Acre (Akko) — 181km (112 miles)
— Ashdod — 66km (41 miles)
— Ashkelon — 73km (45 miles)
— Banais — 227km (141 miles)
— Beer Sheva — 84km (52 miles)
— Bethlehem — 10km (6 miles)
— Beth Shean — 120km (75 miles)
— Eilat — 312km (194 miles)
— Ein Gedi — 163km (101 miles)
— Gaza — 92km (57 miles)
— Haifa — 159km (99 miles)
— Hebron — 35km (22 miles)
— Jericho — 39km (24 miles)
— Lod — 51km (32 miles)
— Metulla — 221km (137 miles)
— Nazareth — 157km (98 miles)
— Netanya — 93km (58 miles)
— Rehovot — 53km (33 miles)
— Rosh Hanikra — 201km (125 miles)
— Safed — 192km (119 miles)
— Shechem — 63km (39 miles)
— Tel Aviv — 62km (38 miles)
— Tiberias — 157km (98 miles)
— Zichron Yaakov — 121km (75 miles)

FOOD

Israeli cuisine is a mixture of dishes from all over the world, because every immigrant has brought some dish, or style of cooking, from his homeland. Kosher food conforms to the Biblical dietary laws prohibiting certain animals, fowl and fish, and forbidding the serving of cream or cheese with meat. But even this has changed with the influx of Jews from Europe who have developed their own style of preparing the food.

Due to the high price, and low quality, of meat, many vegetarian dishes are found on the menu. Dairy products, especially yoghurt, feature prominently.

The most common fast food is felafel, which is pita bread stuffed with fried balls of chickpeas and salad with tehina (sesame) sauce. The next most popular is hummus, which is mashed chickpea with garlic and lemon and pita bread, although to some this will be a little too spicy. Shwarma consists of chunks of roast lamb and salad wrapped in pita bread, and is the staple diet of the Arabs. Shashlik and kebabs are also found everywhere.

Traditional Ashkenzai Jewish cooking includes chopped liver, blintzes, chicken soup and gefilte (stuffed) fish.

There is no shortage of restaurants from other countries, and the cities have their share of Chinese, French, Italian, South American, Hungarian and Indian establishments. American hot dogs and hamburgers have found their way to Israel, too, but they don't seem to taste the same as the originals.

One thing to watch out for is the fact that a restaurant listed as Oriental may not be what you expect. At home, of course, it means Chinese, or maybe even Japanese, Vietnamese, etc, but in Israel it can often mean Middle Eastern, and the food will in no way resemble the kind you eat with chopsticks.

Israeli wines should not be judged by the sickly sweet wines exported to other countries for use on ceremonial occasions. The wine industry is relatively new, and not connected to the ancient winepresses that are at some of the sites. Although there is not a great selection, there is a reasonable Cabernet Sauvignon, and a very light Petite Sirah, and among the whites, the Semillon and the Chenin are worth trying.

Carmel is the largest winery, but others which are making names for themselves are Ben Ami, Montfort and Ashkelon.

Two brands of beer that will be found everywhere are Maccabee and Goldstar. Maccabee is the lighter of the two, and the more expensive.

Tapuzim (orange drink) and eshkoliot (grapefruit drink) are sold everywhere, are cheaper than the fizzy drinks, and much safer than the water.

ENTERTAINMENT

There is no shortage of things to do at night in Israel — cinemas, nightclubs, bars, discos, they're all there, that is if you have the energy after a day spent tramping around ancient sites. All the 'in' places are listed in the section on each city and town.

SHOPPING

Colourful markets and bazaars abound in the old cities of Jerusalem, Bethlehem, Acre, Nazareth and in the Druze villages. As they are really for the locals, wandering through them is a good way to catch the atmosphere of the 'real' Israel. Along with the fruit and vegetables they have a good selection of local handicrafts, especially in leather, bamboo and hand-blown glass.

Beautiful figurines of religious characters, carved in olive wood, are popular souvenirs, as are brass coffee sets, and menorahs (the seven-branched candelabra which is actually the symbol of Israel, and not the Star of David). Other sought-after items are chess sets, backgammon boards and jewellery boxes inlaid with mother-of-pearl.

In the clothing line there is quite a variety of intricately embroidered dresses and shirts, inspired by the different faiths and cultures in Israel, and the workmanship is extremely good. Then, of course, there is the ubiquitous T-shirt, with a variety of scenes and slogans, one favourite being 'Holy Rock Cafe — Jerusalem'.

The main cities have branches of Maskit and WIZO which stock all the native crafts. The Maskit shops are supported by the Ministry of Labour and are outlets for the Maskit home industries programme, providing work for immigrant women. WIZO is sponsored by the Women's International Zionist Organisation.

If you are thinking of splurging on an antique, make sure the shop which contains your treasure has a Ministry of Tourism sticker in the window, otherwise you could be investing in a genuine fake.

SPORT

The most popular spectator sports are soccer and basketball, and there are many international matches during the winter season at stadiums in the Tel Aviv area.

The Mediterranean shoreline and the Sea of Galilee are ideal for swimming, surfing, sailing and water-skiing. The Tel Aviv Marina offers yachting as well as sailing. All the large hotels have swimming pools and there are municipal pools all over the country.

Scuba diving is especially popular along the Gulf of Elait.

Fishing gear can be hired in the Mediterranean and Red Sea areas, though in the latter fishing is permitted only in certain places.

A number of the hotels have tennis courts, and the Tennis Centre at Ramat HaSharon, near Tel Aviv, is putting Israel on the international tennis circuit.

Horseriding clubs are found in Arad, Beersheva, Caesarea, Elait, Netanya and Vered Hagalil.

During the winter there is skiing on the slopes of Mt Hermon.

EMERGENCY ASSISTANCE

Medical assistance is obtainable at all times and most doctors speak English. For emergency or first aid, call on Magen David Adom, the equivalent of the Red Cross by phoning 101 in Jerusalem, Tel Aviv and Haifa.

Emergency hospitals and pharmacies which are open in the evenings, at weekends and on holy days, are listed in the daily newspapers.

Emergency dental treatment is available at weekends and on holy days, in Jerusalem through the Magen David Adom, and in Tel Aviv at 49 Rehov Bar Kokhba.

For police emergencies in Jerusalem, Tel Aviv and Haifa, phone 100.

For fire emergencies in these cities phone 102.

JERUSALEM

The capital city of Israel, and 'Holy City' to one-third of the world's population, Jerusalem is one of very few capitals of the world which does not have a river or sea port.

The word 'Jerusalem' means 'city of peace', which, in view of its turbulent history, is a misnomer, but it does have an atmosphere of tranquilty, and a sense of antiquity. Its people are fiercely patriotic, and extremely proud of their city, whether they are Hasidic Jews with long flowing beards, dressed in long black coats and broad hats, or Arabs with flowing scarves covering their heads.

It is thought that Jerusalem is about 5,000 years old, so it is one of the oldest continuously inhabited cities in the world, yet it is a modern city with a population of around 500,000. The newer parts of the city have been well planned, and being built of sandstone, blend in with the old sections.

After the 1948 Arab-Israeli war, the city was divided, and West Jerusalem (or New Jerusalem) became the Israeli section, and East Jerusalem (or Old Jerusalem) the Jordanian section. This meant that all the religious sites, except for Mount Zion, were in the Jordanian section. There was only one link between the two sections, the Mandelbaum Gate, and non-Jewish visitors could make the crossing once, but could not re-enter Israel, or if they were going the other way, could not re-enter Jordan.

The Six Day War in 1967 saw the Israelis take control of East Jerusalem, and the city was united — theoretically. Even the casual visitor will notice that West Jerusalem has a distinctive Jewish atmosphere, while East Jerusalem is definitely Arab.

The Old City has a Jewish quarter and a Muslim quarter, but there are no restrictions in either quarter for people belonging to the other.

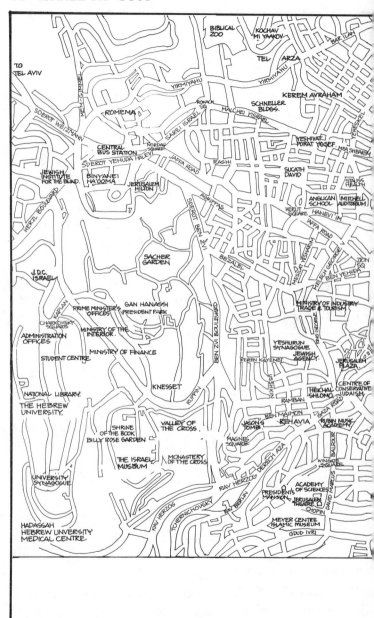

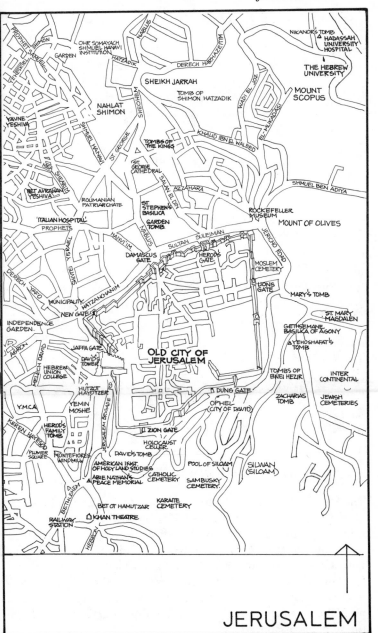

JERUSALEM

HOW TO GET THERE

By Bus

Egged buses no. 945 and 947 have a service from Haifa — Jerusalem, via Ben Gurion Airport, which runs every 40 minutes until 11pm. The fare is 7.00NIS from the airport, and the trip takes 40–45 minutes. The buses do not run on the sabbath.

The service from Egypt to Israel stops first in Tel Aviv, then continues on to Jerusalem, stopping at the Central Bus Station, but will stop at hotels if there are sufficient numbers going to the same hotel.

By Air

There is an airport in Jerusalem, Atarot, but it is not frequently used for travel between Tel Aviv and Jerusalem, most people preferring bus or sherut.

By Sherut

A sherut, with its full complement of 7 passengers, will take you to your hotel in Jerusalem from Ben Gurion Airport, and costs about 10NIS. This fare includes one suitcase.

By Train

The train service from Tel Aviv to Jerusalem is slow and meanders all over the place. When it finally arrives at Jerusalem, take buses nos. 5, 6, 7, 8 or 21 to the city centre.

By car

Jerusalem is 62km from Tel Aviv, on a good, sealed road.

TOURIST INFORMATION

The Israel Government Tourist Information Office has branches at 24 King George Street, ph 241 281, and at the Jaffa Gate in the Old City, ph 282 295. Both offices are open in summer, Sun–Thurs 8.30am–6pm, in winter Sun–Thurs 8.30am–5pm. The King George Street office is closed on Saturday and holidays, but the Jaffa Gate office is open on these days 10am–1pm.

There is also a Christian Information Centre at the Jaffa Gate, ph 287 647, which is open Mon–Sat 8.30am–12.30pm, 3–5.30pm (in summer 3–6pm).

In the Cardo the Jewish Quarter Information Center, ph 281 827, is open for information and advice, Sun–Thurs 9am–6pm, Fri 9am–1pm.

ACCOMMODATION

There's no shortage of accommodation in Jerusalem, and it would be impossible to list it all, so here is a selection with prices in US Dollars for a double room including breakfast, and subject to a 15% service charge. The Telephone Area Code is 02.

5-star Hotels
King David, 23 King David Street, ph 221 111 — $198–240; Sheraton Jerusalem Plaza, 47 King George Street, ph 228 133 — $110–165; Laromme, 3 Jabotinsky Street, ph 697 777 — $120–130; Jerusalem Hilton, Givat Ram, ph 536 151 — $110–125; Moriah Jerusalem, 39 Keren Hayesod Street, ph 232 232 — $105–125; King Solomon, 32 King David Street, ph 241 433 — $105–117; Ramada Renaissance, 6 Wolfson Street, ph 528 111 — $104–110; Inter-Continental, Mt of Olives, ph 282 551 — $90–98; St George International, Salah Eddine Street, ph 282 571 — $52.

4-star Hotels
Mount Zion, 15 Hebron Road, ph 724 222 — $90–110; American Colony, Nablus Road, ph 285 171 — $60–104; Sonesta Jerusalem, 2 Wolfson Street, ph 528 221 — $85–93; Shalom, Beit Vagan, ph 422 111 — $80; Holy Land, Bayit Vegan, ph 630 201 — $90; Ariel, 31 Hebron Road, ph 719 222 — $70; Windmill, 3 Mendele Street, ph 663 111 — $69; Knesset Tower, 4 Wolfson Street, ph 531 111 — $68; Caesar, 208 Jaffa Street, ph 382 156 — $65; Zohar, 47 Leib Jaffe Street, ph 717 557 — $65; National Palace, 4 Az-Zahara Street, ph 273 273 — $55; Jerusalem Panorama, Hill of Gethsemane, ph 284 886 — $52; Capitol, 17 Salah Eddin Street, ph 282 561 — $46; Mount Scopus, 10 Sheikh Jarrah, ph 828 891 —$40; Ambassador, 57 Nablus Road, Sheikh Jarrah, ph 828 211 —$32–42.

3-star Hotels
Jerusalem Tower, 23 Hillel Street, ph 222 161 — $64; Eyal, 21 Shamai Street, ph 234 161 — $60; Reich, 1 Hagai Street, Beit Harkerem, ph 523 121 — $55; YMCA, 26 King David Street,

ph 227 111 — $52; Gloria, Jaffa Gate, ph 282 431 — $45;
Holyland East, 6 Rashid Street, ph 284 841 — $44; Pilgrim's
Palace, Sultan Suleiman Street, ph 284 831 — $44; Jerusalem
Meridian, 5 Ali Ibn Abi Taleb Street, ph 285 212 — $42; Alcazar,
6 Almutanbi Street, ph 281 111 — $40; Strand, 4 Ben Jubeir
Street, ph 280 279 — $40; Neveh Shoshana, 5 Beit Hakerem Street,
ph 521 740 — $39;

2-star Hotels
Palatin, 4 Aggripas Street, ph 231 141 — $46; Ron, 44 Jaffa Street,
ph 223 471 — $46; Victoria, 8 Massoudi Street, ph 286 220 — $36;
Pilgrims Inn, Al Rashid Street, ph 284 883 — $36; Har Aviv, 16 A.
Bet Hakerem Street, ph 521 515 — $36; Lawrence, 18 Salah Eddin
Street, ph 282 585 — $36; Knights Palace, 4 Jawalida Street,
ph 282 537 — $32–36; Metropole, 6 Salah Eddin Street, ph 282
507 — $32; Rivoli, 3 Salah Eddin Street, ph 284 871 — $32;

LOCAL TRANSPORT

Bus
The local bus service is regular, efficient and cheap. A fare of
around 1NIS will cover any route around the city.

Taxi
These can be hailed on the street, picked up at ranks in the main
centres, or booked by phone. The fares are reasonable, but if the
driver won't start his meter make sure you agree on a price before
getting in the car.

Car
Major car rental companies with offices in Jerusalem are:
   Avis, 22 King David Street, ph 249 001.
   Budget, 14 King David Street, ph 226 143.
   Hertz, 18 King David Street, ph 231 351; 27 Saladin Street,
      ph 283 415.
   Hertz also has desks at the Laromme Hotel, ph 697 259; the
      Hilton Hotel, ph 241 949; the Ramada Renaissance Hotel,
      ph 532 915.
   In order to park in the streets of Jerusalem you have to buy a
parking card from newsagents, or at the entrance of large parking
lots. Illegally parked cards have wheel clamps attached by the
police.

NB There is no form of transport in the Old City, so wear
comfortable walking shoes.

EATING OUT

The Old City has a good range of reasonably priced Arab and oriental restaurants, which are open during the sabbath, when the Israeli restaurants are closed. If it is difficult to find a restaurant when you need one, try Umayyah Restaurant, just outside the Old City, across the road from Herod's Gate, which always seems to be open.

Ben Yehuda Street, and the intersecting alleyways, are chock-a-block with cafes, coffee shops, felafel stands and fast-food western-style restaurants.

Yoel Solomon Street, south from Zion Street, has many reasonably-priced places.

Here are a few names and addresses, with prices being the average per person, (not including drinks):

West Jerusalem

Europa, 48 Jaffa Road (near Zion Square), ph 228 953 — kosher —open Sun–Thurs noon-10pm, Fri noon–3pm — under 20NIS.

The Pie House, 5 Hyrcanos Street, ph 242 478 — great pies and salads — open Sun–Thurs 9am–2am, Fri 8am–4pm, Sat 7pm–2am — under 15NIS.

Shemesh, 21 Ben Yehuda Street, ph 222 418 — European/ Eastern — open noon–midnight — 20–40NIS.

Mamma Mia, 18 Rabbi Akiva Street, on Independence Park, ph 248 080 — vegetarian Italian — under 20NIS.

Katy's Restaurant & Bar, 16 Rivlin Street, ph 234 621 — French — closed Friday evening and all Saturday — over 40NIS.

Off The Square, 6 Yoel Salomon Street, ph 242 559 — kosher —open Sun–Thurs noon–midnight, Fri 11am–2pm, Sat sunset–midnight — under 20NIS.

Normans, 9 Yoel Salomon Street, ph 227 444 — steak/hamburger — 20–40NIS.

East Jerusalem

National Palace Restaurant, 4 Al-Zahara Street, ph 282 245 — Middle Eastern — open 7am–10pm, 7 days — 20–40NIS.

Philadelphia, 9 Al-Zahara Street, ph 289 770 — Middle Eastern — open noon–midnight, 7 days — 20–40NIS.

Sea Dolphin, 21 Al-Rashadiah Street, ph 282 788 — seafood — open noon–4pm and 6pm–midnight — 20–40NIS.

Al-Umayyah, Sultan Suleiman Street (between Herod's and Damascus Gates), ph 282 789 — varied menu — open 7 days — under 20NIS.

Macdonalds hasn't made it into Jerusalem (yet) but before you suffer withdrawal symptoms, the local version is MacDavids on Jaffa Road, near Zion Square. But, this branch of the chain is kosher — no cheeseburgers.

ENTERTAINMENT

The Tourist Information Offices have information about cinema and theatre programmes. The *Jerusalem Post* Friday edition lists all types of entertainment, and the hotels have brochures advertising what's on and where. The cinemas are mostly in West Jerusalem, in the vicinity of Zion Square, and are screened in their original language with Hebrew, English or French subtitles. The few cinemas in East Jerusalem show films in Arabic only.

The Sound and Light Show in the Citadel is held in English every evening, except Friday and holidays, from April to October at 8.45, and there is also a show at 10pm on Mon, Tues, Wed and Sat. Tickets are available at the Citadel entrance by the Jaffa Gate. It is advisable to take a jacket, as it is also often cooler there than you would expect.

Many of the big hotels in West Jerusalem have nightclubs, although their floorshows tend to be more cultural than exotic, but after all this is the Holy City. Again the Tourist Information Offices can help.

SHOPPING

The large western-style department stores are on Jaffa Road between Zion Square and Ben Yehuda Street. Of course these are more expensive than bargaining your way through the narrow alleys of the Old City. This area is also the best for quality jewellery shops, such as Idit on Ben Yehuda Street. Maskit in Rav Kook Street, near Zion Square, has very good arts and crafts, fashion and jewellery.

The bazaar in the Old City, is absolutely fascinating. It's a kaleidoscope of colour and a cacophony of sounds amidst a multitude of people. There are no fixed prices, and for that matter, no fixed quality. The best idea is to do a lot of comparison 'window' shopping, and above all get a good night's sleep before you set out.

The Way of the Cross passes through the Arab quarter. I have nothing against shopping, but having someone extol the virtues of their wares in your ear when you are gazing in awe at the various Stations of the Cross along the Via Dolorosa, is, to say the least, off-putting. So if you are serious about the religious sites, I suggest you make two trips — one for your soul, and one for your souvenirs.

Next to the Sixth Station is Jerusalem Pottery, which stocks the best Armenian pottery, and next door is the Benevolent Arts, with fine quality embroidered clothes and table linen.

In comparison, the Jewish quarter (on the way to the Wailing Wall) is a staid shopping experience, with clean shops in clean arcades, and higher prices. In the Cardo there are exclusive boutiques offering leather and fur goods, and excellent art galleries.

There are very good craft shops in Hutzot Hayotzer, outside and below the Jaffa Gate, and at the Jerusalem House of Quality, 12 Hebron Road, close to the Railway Station, behind St Andrew's Church.

SIGHTSEEING

THE OLD CITY
Surrounded by 16th century walls built by Suleiman the Magnificent, the one square kilometre (220 acres) of the Old City contains some of the holiest sites of the three major religions of the world. It is divided into five sections: the Christian Quarter, the Moslem Quarter, the Jewish Quarter, the Armenian Quarter and Temple Mount.

The walls have eight gates — Golden Gate and Lions' (St Stephen's) Gate on the eastern side; New Gate, Damascus Gate and Herod Gates on the northern; Jaffa Gate on the western; Dung Gate and Zion Gate on the southern.

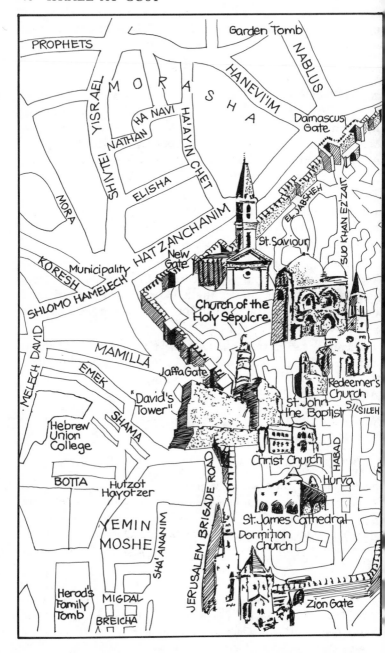

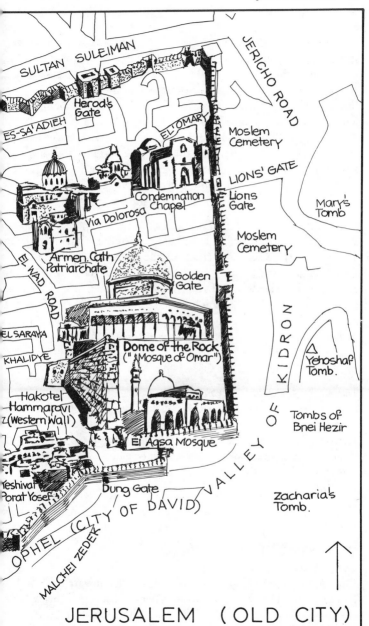

JERUSALEM   (OLD CITY)

Golden Gate

In the eastern wall are what seem to be double gates sealed with stones. It is thought that this is the gate referred to by Ezekiel when he said the gate would stay shut until the prince came. (Ezekiel 44:1–3). Jewish tradition says that the Messiah will enter Jerusalem through this gate, and Christians believe that the gate will remain closed until Jesus Christ returns. However, Israeli archaeologist Meir Ben-Dov, who has carried out many excavations in the Old City, believes that the gate was not built until the Islam era, and could not have been there in Ezekiel's time. He thinks it was built as a commemorative victory gate, maybe to celebrate Muhammad's arrival at the mount.

Jaffa Gate

A pair of medieval towers, which are part of the Citadel of David and the most convenient entry to the Old City from the New City, the gate was built by Suleiman the Magnificent in 1538. The road from here leads to Jaffa on the Mediterranean Sea. The Arabs, however, know it as the Hebron Gate, because the road to that city, where Abraham is buried, also starts here. A branch of the Tourist Information is just inside the entrance, and nearby are two graves, believed to belong to Suleiman's architects, who may not have died from natural causes.

Damascus Gate and Herod's Gate

Both these gates lead into the Muslim (or Arab) Quarter. The Damascus Gate is so called because it led to the old road from Jerusalem to Damascus. It is the most beautiful of the gates, and to the left is an arch of the Roman entrance gate to Aelia Capitolina, the city built by Emperor Hadrian.

Lions' Gate (or St Stephen's Gate)

The outside of the gate has carved reliefs of animals that look much more like panthers than lions, but in any case, this is the closest gate to the beginning of the Way of the Cross.

Dung Gate

Opening near the Western or Wailing Wall, the gate is also quite handy to the Dome of the Rock. There are several stories about the name, the most popular being that the rubbish tip was in the vicinity.

Wailing Wall (Men's Section), Jerusalem

The 'Old City', Jerusalem showing the Wailing Wall & Dome of the Rock

Looking from the Old City to the Mount of Olives in the New City, Jerusalem

Zion Gate
Connects the Armenian Quarter with Mt Zion.

New Gate
As the name implies, this gate was not built until 1887 when the growth of modern Jerusalem necessitated a gate to serve the new settlements. It was built by Sultan Abdul Hamid II.

It is possible to walk on the ramparts of the walls, starting at the Jaffa, Damascus, Lion's and Zion Gates, and this is the best way to understand their military importance. There is a fee for the walk, but the tickets are good for 48 hours, so you can do it in stages over the two days if you like. The entire walk (the Temple Mount area is closed) is about 4km (2.5 miles), and make sure you have plenty of film, remember your water bottle, and ignore all the local 'guides' who will offer to show you special things. Unfortunately, it is necessary to advise women not to walk the ramparts on their own, as there have been some nasty incidents.

If you would rather join a group contact the Tourist Information Office (ph 228 844) who can advise you on the various walking tours that are available.

THE CITADEL
The Citadel of David can be reached either through Jaffa Gate, or an entrance just to the right of the Gate. The Tower of David is the tallest structure in the Citadel, but as it is actually a Turkish minaret, the name seems a bit incongruous. The other large tower here is the only survivor of three built by Herod the Great, but archaeologists haven't been able to establish the sites of the other two.

Much excavation has been carried out, and the courtyard of the Citadel has been exposed, showing the different periods of occupation. It is now a cultural centre with open-air concerts in summer, and the sound and light show in the evenings (see Entertainment section for times). Also in the Citadel is the Municipal Museum, which has an exhibition of cultural and religious dress throughout the ages, and an audio-visual presentation of history and life of the city.

The Citadel is open Sat–Thurs 8.30am–4pm, Fri 8.30am–2pm, and there is a small admission fee.

Across from the moat entrance to the Citadel is the oldest Anglican Church in the Middle East, Christ Church, built in 1849.

ARMENIAN QUARTER

Occupied by these staunch Christians since very early times, the Armenian Quarter has many ancient buildings, including St James Cathedral and the Church of the Holy Archangels. The Cathedral is only open during afternoon services.

Bazaar

If you stay on David Street after coming through the Jaffa Gate you will find yourself in the middle of the bazaar (suq in Arabic, shuk in Hebrew). David Street becomes Street of the Chain after a while, which leads to the Wailing Wall and the Gate of the Chain entrance to Temple Mount. Sounds easy doesn't it? It looks easy on the map, too, but in practice its an obstacle course. There are signs along the way pointing out the direction to the Wall, but you'll still get the feeling you are lost in a maze of narrow walkways, filled with people, donkeys, shops with their spruikers, and the ever-present smell of all the above and innumerable spices. Of course you can pick up a bargain or three along the way, but be careful of those 'genuine' antiquities.

WESTERN WALL

The Second Temple was built in 516BC when the Jews returned from exile. It was rebuilt by Herod in 20BC, and destroyed by Titus, the Roman general, in 70AD, as Christ had predicted (Matthew 24:2). A portion of the retaining wall around the Temple remains today, and it is known as the Western, or Wailing Wall. It is the holiest of the Jewish sites, and is called Wailing, because the Jews are still lamenting the loss of their Temple.

After the Six Day War in 1967, the Jewish people tore down the alley ways in front of the Wall, and built a large plaza to accommodate the hundreds of pilgrims and tourists who flock to the Wall daily. The Wall has the same rules as an Orthodox synagogue, so the prayer areas for men and women are separated by a screen. The Torah scrolls are kept in the connecting buildings on the men's side of the Wall.

The Wall is always accessible, and men must have head coverings, and women must not have bare shoulders. Skull caps and shawls are available, free of charge. Photography is permitted except on the Sabbath, when services are held.

Whatever your religion, it is impossible not to feel moved by the sight of the Wall, with its paper supplications stuffed in the cracks, and the Orthodox Jews in their black clothes praying so fervently at its base. Bar-Mitzvahs are held here and are very moving ceremonies at this sacred spot.

TEMPLE MOUNT

The steps to the right of the Western Wall lead to Temple Mount, Mount Moriah. David bought the flat rock on top of Mount Moriah from Ornan the Jesubite, who had used it as threshing-floor, for six hundred shekels of gold (1 Chron. 21:25). Solomon used the same site to build the First Temple (2 Chron. 3:1), and when it was destroyed the Second Temple which was enlarged by Herod, replaced it.

What we see today is a stone-paved area of about 12ha (30 acres) with two mosques and the Islamic Museum, which are open 8.30–11am, 12.15–3pm and 4–5pm. Both mosques are closed to visitors on Friday and Moslem holidays. At a ticket box nearby you can buy a ticket for 10NIS which includes admission to the mosques and the museum. Incidently, religious Orthodox Jews won't go anywhere near here in case they accidently step on the Holy of Holies.

El Aqsa Mosque

The present mosque, built in 1034, is actually the second built on this site, the first being destroyed by earthquake. During the Crusades it was used as a Christian church, but when Saladin conquered Jerusalem, El Aqsa returned to being a mosque.

Of course, it is necessary to remove your shoes when you enter, but unfortunately the people in charge make you leave your shoes quite a distance away, so you spend your time in the mosque wondering whether you will have to take in the rest of the Old City barefooted. Anyway, the interior of the mosque is beautiful, with marble columns, colourful painted ceilings, priceless carpets and glorious stained glass windows. There is a wood-partitioned platform at the end of the columns reserved for King Hussein when he comes to pray. The right-hand side of the mosque is the women's prayer area, and the locals prefer women tourists to stick to that area too.

Outside the mosque, at the far end of the paved area is a corner of the city walls. This may be, some believe, the 'pinnacle of the Temple' where Satan took Christ to tempt him (Matthew 4:5), but even if it's not, there is a very good view of the Mount of Olives, the Kidron Valley and the Garden of Gethsemane.

Near here there is a stairway leading to underground chambers called Solomon's Stables. You have to find a guide (or he will find you) and pay an extra fee to see this cavern, and frankly I don't think it is worth it.

Dome of the Rock

Across the open paved space between the two mosques is the El-Kas fountain, where Muslims perform their ablutions before entering the holy places.

Then there is the Dome of the Rock, the most beautiful building in Jerusalem. The outside, which has been beckoning all the time with its gold roof, is breathtaking, and the interior well and truly lives up to expectations. Many of the tiles on the external walls were laid during the time of Suleiman the Magnificent, and those that did not stand the test of time were replaced by Hussein of Jordan. Unfortunately, it is fairly easy to pick which is which, so that's another ancient art that has been lost. Also I have to tell you that the roof is no longer pure gold, but an aluminium bronze alloy, but who cares, it still looks like gold.

As you enter the mosque you will first be astounded by the carpets, then the huge wooden fence around 'The Rock' (which you can slip you hands through to touch the hard cold stone), then the incredible stained glass windows and black and gold mosaics. A person will wander up to you and explain all about the building, how this was where Muhammad went to heaven, how they still have some of his hair in a tabernacle, but he won't mention that this was where Abraham built his sacrificial altar, or that the Temple of Solomon was built around the rock. To him this is strictly a Muslim holy place, because Muhammad said that one prayer at this rock was worth a thousand anywhere else.

The rock, by the way, is about 9m by 9m, and rises about 2m above the floor. There is a stairway leading under the rock to a cave where people go to pray, which incidentally is as hot an oven.

JEWISH QUARTER

The quarter was reclaimed by the Israelis in 1976 after the Six Day War, and since then there has been a lot of building and reconstruction. It extends from the Western Wall to Habạd Street.

The Old Yishuv Court Museum, 6 Rehov Or Hayyim, ph 284 636, gives an insight into the life of the Jewish community living here before the destruction in 1948. Open Sun–Thurs 9am–4pm, admission fee.

The Ramban Synagogue on Rehov HaYehudim was built by Rabbi Moshe Nahmanides in 1267, and is the oldest still standing. Next to it are the ruins of the Hurva Synagogue, built on the ruins of the 13th century Crusader Church of St Martin. Rabbi Yehuda the Hasid led his Polish followers to the Holy Land in 1699 and began construction of the Hurva, but it was not completed until 1864, and then destroyed in 1948.

The Four Sephardic Synagogues — the synagogues of Rabbi Yohanan Ben Zakkai and of Eliyahu HaNavi, the Central Synagogue and the Stambouli Synagogue — were built by Spanish exiles in the 16th century. To conform with a Muslim law forbidding synagogues to be taller than surrounding buildings, the synagogues were built in large chambers under the ground. They are still the spiritual centre of Jerusalem's Sephardic community, with services held every morning and evening.

The Cardo

Meaning the 'heart', the Cardo was the main street in Roman and Byzantine Jerusalem. It has recently been excavated and restored. Under the new vaulted roof are boutiques and art galleries, but the uncovered section is built over an extension of Emperor Hadrian's Cardo Maximus which ran from Damascus gate.

It's actually quite a strange mixture. In front of a shop selling exotic furs and leathers there is a hole in the ground showing the remains of an old city below.

There are steps down to an excavated section of Hasmonean city walls and remains of some buildings from the First Temple Period, near the entrance to the Cardo.

VIA DOLOROSA (The Way of the Cross)

From the Lion's Gate a short walk takes you to the Church of St Anne on the right. The church is the purest example of Crusader architecture still standing in Jerusalem, and is built on the site of the birthplace of Mary, Jesus' mother. Her parents, St Anne and St Joachim, lived here and there is a grotto underneath the church were Mary was born. The church survived the Mamluk period because it was used as a Muslim theological school.

In the grounds of the church is the Pool of Bethesda, where sacrificial sheep were washed before being taken to the Temple, and where Jesus cured the crippled man (John 5:2–9). Excavations have revealed the original steps, hidden beneath Byzantine and Crusader churches.

At the Franciscan monastery, which is actually Station II, it is possible to find a monk who will be willing to act as a guide (for free) for the Via Dolorosa, which they normally do on a Friday afternoon, and have been doing since the 15th century. If that doesn't work, you will probably be able to pick up a licensed guide near Station I, failing that there is bound to be a local who will help out, but remember to settle on a price first.

Station I
Jesus is Condemned to Death. The Way of the Cross commences at the El-Omariyeh College, which is the possible site of Pontius Pilate's judgment hall, where Jesus was condemned.

Station II
Jesus Takes Up His Cross. Opposite the College is the Franciscan monastery, to the left of the entrance is the Condemnation Chapel, and on the right is the Chapel of Flagellation. There is a crown of thorns on the dome.

The Via Dolorosa then continues and passes beneath the Ecce Homo Arch where tradition says Pilate looked down at Jesus and said "Behold the Man". The Arch is actually part of a larger arch commemorating Hadrian's suppression of the Bar Kohba revolt in the 2nd century.

Station III
Jesus Falls the First Time. A small Polish chapel on Al-Wad Road to the left, marks the spot where He fell, and there is a relief above the entrance depicting the event.

Station IV
Jesus Meets His Mother. There is also a small chapel here, a few metres from Station III and just past the Armenian Orthodox Patriarchate.

Station V
Simon of Cyrene carries Jesus' Cross. At the next corner there is a small 19th century Franciscan oratory commemorating Simon's deed.

Station VI
Veronica Wipes the Face of Jesus. Turn right from Station V and walk half-way up the street, this is where a woman stepped up to Jesus, wiped His face, and His image was preserved on the cloth. Veronica means 'true image', and although the woman has since come to be known as St Veronica, her actual identity is unknown.

Station VII
Jesus Falls the Second Time. At the top of the hill is the spot where this most likely happened.

Station VIII
Jesus Consoles the Women of Jerusalem. To the left and up a side-street there is 'VIII' carved into the stone, and a Latin cross. This is where Jesus told the women they should weep for themselves and their children rather than for him (Luke 23:28).

Station IX
Jesus Falls the Third Time. The exact location of this station is in dispute. Some say that it is a pillar about 100m past Station VIII at the end of a ramp. Others believe it is in the Ethiopian Convent, which is built on the roof of the Holy Sepulchre. A column embedded in the wall is the spot they choose. In any case, the Convent is worth a visit, and is the only part of the Church that the Copts, one of the world's oldest Christian communities, can claim.

The Way of the Cross now leads into the Church of the Holy Sepulchre, which has the final five stations.

Station X
Jesus is Stripped of His Garments. After entering the church take the steps to the right. The chapel at the top is divided into two naves. The right belongs to the Franciscans, the left to the Greek

Orthodox. At the entrance to the Franciscan Chapel, on a platform resting on the rock of Golgotha, is Station X.

Station XI
Jesus is Nailed to the Cross. At the far end of the Franciscan chapel.

Station XII
Jesus Dies on the Cross. In the Greek chapel there is an altar, with enormous candles, stacks of flowers and a life-size crucifix. Under the altar is a hole and a silver disk marking the place where Jesus' cross was set up.

Station XIII
Jesus is laid in the Arms of His Mother. Between the Franciscan and Greek chapels (that is between Stations XI and XII) is a small shrine with a wooden statue of Mary covered with jewels, with a dagger in her breast. Under the statue is a part of the original rock.

Station XIV
Jesus is Laid in the Tomb. Back on the ground floor of the church, and to your left if you were entering the church, is the Holy Sepulchre in the centre of the rotunda. It is surrounded by gigantic candles. The first chamber in the tomb is the Chapel of the Angel who announced Jesus' resurrection to Mary Magdalene. A small door in this chapel leads into a very small room (it can only hold 6 people at a time) containing the stone shelf on which Jesus' body lay, only it is now covered with marble. To the right of the Sepulchre, is the Chapel of Mary Magdalene, on the place where Jesus appeared to her after the resurrection.

CHURCH OF THE HOLY SEPULCHRE
It was Queen Helena, mother of Constantine, who decided that this site was Golgotha (Hebrew for 'skull', in Latin — Calvary), the spot where Christ had been crucified, when she visited Jerusalem in 326AD. She organised excavations which uncovered the tomb of Joseph of Arimathea, and Constantine built the first church on the site in 335AD. This church was destroyed by the Persians in 614, it was rebuilt, then destroyed by the Turks in 1009, and the Crusaders built the present church in the 12th century.

It is fairly obvious when entering the church that the Crusaders did not really have a plan, it seems the building just evolved, and it now needs a lot of restoration. In fact, a good clean-up would do wonders. The church is, in a word, depressing, not because of what happened there, but because of the derelict state of what is the holiest place in Christendom. The fact that it is controlled by five different religions — Roman Catholic, Armenian Orthodox, Greek Orthodox, Abyssinian Coptic, Syrian Orthodox — doesn't help matters much. They have literally come to blows about who owns what, so nobody does anything, except when there is danger of some part collapsing.

Apart from the holy sites mentioned in The Way of the Cross, there is the Stone of Unction, just opposite the entrance to the church, where Jesus body was prepared for burial, and in the Armenian Section there is a part of the true cross.

While the above religions are arguing over ownership of the Church of the Holy Sepulchre, the Protestant religion has its own idea about where Christ was crucified. A few hundred metres north of the Damascus Gate, outside the Old City, is a hill whose rock-face closely resembles a skull, and in 1883 the British General Gordon, put forward the theory that this was Golgotha (or Calvary). The site was purchased in 1894, and subsequent excavation revealed an ancient tomb, a garden with water cistern, wine-press, and other elements of the records of the death, burial and resurrection of Christ. Called *The Garden Tomb*, it is in a lane off Nablus Road, and is open to the public. There is always someone there to show you around this peaceful part of East Jerusalem, but you'll have to make up your own mind as to which religion has got it right.

OUTSIDE THE WALLS

MOUNT ZION

The Mount is south of the old city, opposite Zion Gate, and is home to several impressive structures including King David's Tomb and the Dormition Abbey.

The building with the tower is the *Dormition Abbey*, the site of the assumption into heaven of the Virgin Mary. The present building was completed in 1910, but of course there were several earlier memorials on the spot. The sanctuary of the abbey has beautiful mosaics in the Byzantine style, but the crypt beneath the sanctuary is the main part. This is where Mary spent her last days on earth, and there is a figurine of her on display. The abbey is not open to visitors between noon and 2pm.

Opposite the Dormition Abbey is the *Tomb of King David*. This is another place that causes some controversy. The walls of the City of David, that is Jerusalem about 1000BC, did not encompass Mount Zion, so the archaeologists tell us, and the Bible tells us that David was buried in the City of David (1 Kings 2:10), so maybe this is not the correct place for David's Tomb. But, does it matter? For centuries Jewish pilgrims have prayed here, and the end results have probably been the same. Open Sun–Thurs 9am–5pm, Fri 9am–2pm.

In the same building, on the floor above, is the *Coenaculum* (dining room) which most Christians believe is the room where Christ shared his Last Supper with his Apostles. The room now is bare, not ornate as in the famous painting by Leonardo da Vinci, so perhaps this is the only holy site in Jerusalem that is not now as elaborate as it was originally. Up a few stairs from this room is another which is considered by some to be the place where the apostles gathered after Jesus' death and received the Holy Spirit. Open 9am–5pm.

Directly opposite the Tomb of David is the *Chamber of the Holocaust* (open Sun–Thurs 8am–5pm, Fri 8am–2pm), which is in memory of the millions of Jews killed in the Holocaust during World War II. It is a very moving memorial, with displays of horrendous artifacts, but it should be seen so no-one will ever forget.

KIDRON VALLEY

The Kidron Valley is also known as the Valley of Jehoshaphat, and runs between Temple Mount and the Mount of Olives. It contains the *Gihon Spring*, which was the city's water supply in ancient times, and also was the means of David capturing the city (see Israel — History section). King Hezekiah made sure that David's way of entry could not be repeated when he built an aquaduct to bring the water into the city and store it in the *Pool of Siloam*. The aquaduct, known as Hezekiah's Tunnel, is still there, and if you don't mind walking through water about 50cm deep, you can paddle along it, but please wear something on your feet. It's best to start at the Gihon Spring source on Shiloah Way and walk to the Pool. It takes about half an hour and a flashlight comes in very handy.

The Pool of Siloam is mentioned in the Bible as the place where Jesus cured the blind man (John 9:6–11).

In the Valley there are many tombs and gravestones, some recent (only a century old) but one appears to date back to the Second Temple period. It is though to be the *Tomb of Absalom*, David's favourite son (2 Sam. 18:18).

The Valley of Jehoshaphat is also mentioned in the Bible (Joel 3:2,12). It will be here that the judgements will be made on Resurrecton Day. Muslims have a similar belief that all the righteous will be saved and the rest will perish in the Valley of Jehoshaphat.

Near the Tomb of Absalom is *Zechariah's Tomb*, which has been carved out of the rock, and has a pyramid-shaped roof. The problem is — which Zechariah? The prophet or the father of John the Baptist?

MOUNT OF OLIVES

The best view of the Old City is from the top of the Mount of Olives, but if you intend to walk up to the summit, do it early in the morning before it gets too hot. On the summit is the small, insignificant *Chapel of the Ascension*, which is in the grounds of a small mosque. Inside the chapel is a footprint, which is said to belong to Christ. Most Christians go along with this as the site of the Ascension, except the Russian Orthodox who believe it happened where they have built the Russian Church of the Ascension, just up the street.

South of the Chapel is the *Pater Noster Church*, where it is thought Jesus taught his disciples the Lord's Prayer (Pater Noster). The present church was built during the late 19th century, and on the inside walls the Lord's Prayer is written in over 40 languages. Next to the church is the tomb of Eleona, the Princess de la Tour d'Auvaigne, who financed the reconstruction of the site. On the adjoining hill are the Carmelite Convent and the Basilica of the Sacred Heart.

On the path that goes down the Mount of Olives from the Intercontinental Hotel, is the *Tomb of the Prophets*, supposed to the burial place of Zechariah, Malachi and Haggai, but of course someone has 'proven' that the tombs are not old enough. Anyway, they are open Sun–Fri, 8am–3pm.

Further down is the *National Cemetery* and the *Common Grave* of those who were killed in 1948 fighting for the Jewish Quarter. Below and behind them is the oldest Jewish Cemetery in the world. When Jews come to the Holy Land to die, this is where they want to be buried, because they believe it is closest to Heaven.

To the right of the Tomb of the Prophets there is a path leading to *Dominus Flevit* (open 8–11.30am, 3–5pm), a Franciscan church built where Jesus wept over Jerusalem (Luke 19:41–44). Continue down the path and you are in the *Garden of Gethsemane*, which is shared by the various denominations, like the Church of the Holy Sepulchre. First church you come to is the Russian *Church of Mary Magdalene*. The seven golden onion-shaped domes really stand out in any photograph of the Mount of Olives, and the church is really beautiful. It was built by Tsar Alexander III and dedicated to his mother Empress Maria Alexandrovna, but the body in the crypt is that of Russian Grand Duchess Elizabeth. The church is now a convent, and is open to visitors Tues and Thurs 9am–noon, 2–4pm.

The end of the path brings you to the *Basilica of the Agony* (Church of All Nations), and you have to enter through the gate on the left below the Church of Mary Magdalene. Behind an iron door is a garden which most think (others think somewhere else — two other places actually) is where Jesus spent his last night and was betrayed by Judas (Mark 14:32–42). The olive grove here is accepted as one of the oldest in the world, but don't let anyone tell you that the trees are the same ones that were there in the time of Christ — olive trees just don't live that long. The church here was built after World War I, by donations from all over the world (hence the name) but the site has been recognised since the 4th century. On the facade of the church is a beautiful mosaic depicting Jesus bringing peace to all nations. The garden and church are open 8.30am–noon and 3pm–sunset April–October, 8.30am–12 noon and 2pm–sunset November–March. Incidentally, Gethsemane means oilpress.

Turn right at the foot of the road ahead of the church and you come to the *Tomb of Mary* in an underground cavern (open 6.30am–noon, 2–5pm). Some say this is the site of Mary's death and assumption into heaven, and it is such a gloomy place that it is quite easy to believe that someone died here, but the Dormition Abbey on Mount Zion is more likely to have been the site of the Assumption.

EAST JERUSALEM

Prior to 1967 East Jerusalem was the commercial centre of Jordanian-controlled Jerusalem, and it is still principally Arab. As the Muslim Sabbath starts on sunset Thursday and continues until sunset Friday, shops in this area are closed for this period, and restaurants will not serve alcohol.

Halfway between Herod's and Damascus Gates, on Suleiman Street, are *Solomon's Quarries*, from which the stone for the Second Temple was quarried. The caves extend about 250m underneath the Old City, and legend has it that the last King of Judeah, Zedekiah, escaped from the invading army of King Nebuchadnezzer of Babylon through a passage connecting the caves to the royal palace. They are open Sun–Thurs, 9am–5pm, Fri 9am–3pm, and there is an admission fee.

Also on Suleiman Street is the *Rockefeller Archeological Museum*, arguably the best museum in Jerusalem. Its exhibits trace man from the Iron Age, through the Biblical, Greek and Roman periods to the present day. One of the most fascinating items is the skeleton of Mount Carmel Man, who lived around 100,000 years ago. The museum is open Sun–Thurs 10am–5pm, Fri–Sat 10am–2pm.

From Suleiman Street turn right up Nablus Road and follow the signs to the *Garden Tomb* (see section on Church of the Holy Sepulchre for history) The tomb is open Mon–Sat 8am–noon, 2.30–5pm and there is an entrance fee.

Further up Nablus Road is *St George's Cathedral*, which was consecrated in 1898, and is part of the British-owned Christ Church, but has an Arab bishop.

Past the cathedral, near the corner of Saladin Street, are the *Tombs of the Kings*, which were thought to contain the remains of the Judean kings, but have now been proven to be the tomb of the family of Queen Helena of Adiabene (on the border of Persia). She converted to Judaism, and came to Jerusalem to live, and die.

Stay on Nablus Road, passing the American Colony Hotel and the Sheikh Jarrah Mosque, then turn right, then left and you come to the *Tomb of Simon the Just*, who was a high priest during the Second Temple period. Although there is some doubt (what's new?) that this is actually Simon's tomb, Orthodox Jews venerate the site. North-east of the tomb is *Mount Scopus*, from which there are some of the best views of the whole of Jerusalem. Although the area remained in Israeli territory, in 1948 the Hebrew University and the Hadassah Hospital closed down and relocated in Western Jerusalem. Since 1967, both institutions have been reopened. The university library is Israel's National Library.

WEST JERUSALEM

The area west of Damascus Gate and Nablus Road is the political and commercial centre of Jerusalem. Prior to 1860, everybody lived inside the walls of the Old City, and when communities were first established outside, the people were not too keen to leave the safety of the locked gates. The first housing development, necessary as the Jewish Quarter of the Old City was becoming extremely congested, was Mishkenot Sha'ananim (Dwellings of Tranquility). It is now a guest house run by the Jerusalem Foundation for visiting artists, musicians and writers. Adjacent is *Yemin Moshe*, an up-market area which used to be an artists' colony. There is a windmill on King David Street which has been turned into a museum dedicated to Sir Moses Montefiore, the British philanthropist who founded the Mishkenot Sha'ananim (open Sun–Fri 4–7pm, Sat 10am–1pm).

North of the windmill and just off King David Street is *Herod's Family Tomb*, in which members of his family are buried, but not Herod himself (he was buried at the Herodion, south of Bethlehem). The tomb is open Mon–Thurs 10am–1pm and there is an entrance fee.

Zahal Square, at the western-most corner of the Old City a few steps from New Gate, is the beginning of West Jerusalem. Across the street is the *Notre Dame de France*, built in 1887 as a hospice and monastery, and now a hostel for pilgrims.

Russian Compound

Near the Central Post Office, on Jaffa Road, is the Russian Compound, which includes a green-domed Russian Orthodox church. The Israelis once rented some of the area for administrative offices, then finally purchased the compound from Russia in 1965. In the Hall of Heroism, which was once the Central Prison, is a permanent exhibit of Jewish underground activities prior to 1948. The cells and execution chambers are also open for visitors, daily 10am–4pm.

Zion Square

The heart of West Jerusalem, Zion Square is further along Jaffa Road where it meets Ben Yehuda Street. The open-air mall of Ben Yehuda Street is a popular meeting place for the locals with its array of shops and eating places.

Salomon Street runs off Zion Square and leads to *Nahalat Shiva*, one of the 19th century neighbourhoods, with its alley-ways of old houses and courtyards.

The marketplace of *Mahane Yehuda* (Judah's Camp) is about 50m from Zion Square on Jaffa Road. This food market is particularly busy on Thursdays and Fridays with the locals buying up for the Sabbath, when everything around here is closed. Further along Jaffa Road is the Central Bus Station where buses leave for all parts of the city and the rest of the country. Opposite is the Binyanai Ha-Ooma, the concert hall for the Israel Philharmonic Orchestra.

Mea She'arim

North of Zion Square is the quarter called Mea She'arim, which is home to the mystical Hasidic sect of Orthodox Jews. Mea She'arim means 'hundredfold' and comes from the Book of Genesis (26:12): "Then Isaac sowed in that land, and reaped in the same year a hundredfold; and the Lord blessed him."

A visit to this quarter will take you back in time. You will see long-bearded men in black gowns, and either beaver-fur hats or broad-brimmed black hats, young boys with side-curls, and married women wearing wigs and scarves to cover their shaven heads. Shops selling religious ornaments abound, and there are dozens of Talmudic schools and synagogues. The people are so Orthodox that they frequently clash with authorities, believing that modern Israel is a blasphemous society. Many of the locals only speak Yiddish amongst themselves, for they believe that Hebrew is too sacred for everyday use.

Visitors are reminded that they should dress modestly, and women should wear long skirts — trousers are not allowed. Also, you can forget about taking lots of photographs as most of the inhabitants are totally against having their photo taken. But apart from that, you are free to wander around, and even visit the synagogues.

Prophets Street
The Christian Street of West Jerusalem, Rehov Hanevi'im has many missionary societies and foreign churches, and can be reached by any of the streets heading north from Zion Square. Among them are the Swedish Theological Seminary, the Christian Missionary Alliance, the American Bible Institute and the Abyssinian Church.

Jewish Agency
From Zion Square, take Ben Yehuda Street, then turn left into King George V Street. In this street are the Jewish Agency headquarters, Keren Kayemet (Jewish National Fund) and Keren Hayesod (United Israel Appeal). The Jewish Agency building was badly damaged by a bomb just before the establishment of the state. There are several displays in the compound, and free films about Israel are shown occasionally. Enquire at the Tourist Information Office.

Heichal Shlomo
On King George V Street is Heichal Shlomo, seat of the chief Rabbis and the Great Synagogue. The building is of the style of King Solomon's Temple, square at the base with domes on top, and free tours are available Sun–Thurs 9am–1pm, Fri 9am–noon. For information about special programmes, contact the Tourist Information Office.

Independence Park
Opposite Heichal Shlomo, in King George V Street is Jerusalem's Independence Park. At the eastern end of the park is the Mamilla Pool, which is thought to be part of the Old City's ancient water system. Nearby is a small Muslim cemetery.

Tourists at the Via Dolorosa, Jerusalem

Cable Car up to Masada

Sachne Springs in Lower Galilee

The YMCA

The 46m oriental tower of the YMCA offers an extremely good view over Jerusalem. The 'Y' was built in 1928 from the generous donation of New Jersey millionaire, James Jarvie, and has the city's first swimming pool. It also has tennis courts, lecture hall, gymnasium and an archeological museum, the Herbert E. Clark Collection of Near Eastern Antiquities, with a wide range of exhibits. There are also organ recitals every Saturday at 11.30am.

King David Hotel

Built in 1930 across the street from the YMCA, the King David Hotel was the city's first grand hotel. In 1946, the entire south wing was bombed because it was a meeting-place for British Protectorate personnel. It has been totally reconstructed. It is an old-worlde hotel, full of atmosphere, and a great place to have that leisurely drink.

A couple of hundred metres south of the hotel is the Liberty Bell Garden, which has an exact replica of the Liberty Bell of Philadelphia.

OUTLYING ATTRACTIONS

The Knesset

Israel's Parliament is an impressive modern building of peach-coloured stone. It is actually the third Parliament building, and the first permanent one. The first was a converted cinema in Tel Aviv, and the second a converted bank at the corner of King George V Avenue and Ben Yehuda Street, where the Government Tourist offices are now.

There are guided tours of the building on Sunday and Thursday from 8.30am–2.30pm, and visitors must carry their passport. It is also possible to attend a session of parliament on Monday, Tuesday or Wednesday from 4–9pm (except on Jewish holidays and in summer, when parliament is in recess). Take Bus 24, 28 or 99 from Central Bus Station.

Greek Monastery of The Cross

The monastery is over a thousand years old, but legend has it that the trees that once grew here were planted by Lot after he fled Sodom, and that one of them was used to make Jesus' cross. I don't know how people can get excited about trees that don't exist anymore, or for that matter, how they can know what trees grew here that long ago?

Israel Museum

Located south of the Knesset on Ruppin Street, the museum is actually a collection of museums. There is the Bezalel Art Museum, the Samuel Bronfman Biblical and Archeological Museum, the Billy Rose Art Garden and the Shrine of the Book.

The most impressive building is the white-dome structure of the Shrine of the Book, which is designed to look like the lids of the jars in which the Dead Sea Scrolls were stored. (See section on Qumran for more information on Dead Sea Scrolls.) The interior of the Shrine is a series of underground caves, exhibiting documents dating back 2000 years. In the circular chamber are the famous Dead Sea Scrolls. They are in glass cases, and each case has a switch which turns on a light so that you can read the translation and try to make out some of the ancient inscriptions. Everyone realises that precautions must be taken to preserve the documents, but these lights were installed by someone who had obviously taken a speed-reading course, and graduated with honours. You 'literally' get tired of switching on the light, with the result that you start to get bored. Nevertheless, they shouldn't be missed.

In the main buildings of the Museum are the Bronfman and Bezalel collections. The former has a vast array of archaeological exhibits dating from the Early Stone Age to the Middle Ages, and the latter is an extremely fine collection of modern painting and sculpture, mostly from Israel, but it does includes others such as Rembrandt, Picasso and Soutine.

In the Billy Rose Art Garden, which covers 8ha (20 acres), there are both classical and modern Israeli, European and American works.

Make sure you allow plenty of time to spend in the complex, as there is certainly a lot to see. The museum is open Sun, Mon, Wed, Thurs 10am–5pm, Tues 4–10pm, Fri–Sat 10am–2pm, with free guided tours on Mon, Wed, Thurs, Fri, Sun at 11 am, and on Tues at 4.30pm. Take Bus 9, 17, 24. Entrance fee, including Shrine of the Book is 9NIS. There is a gift shop in the main building, and a moderately-priced cafeteria outside, to the right of the stairs.

Mount Herzl

Theodor Herzl was the founder of the modern Zionist Movement, and his tomb is in a pleasant park at the end of the Bet Hakerem section. Herzl was a prolific playwright, and as a newspaper correspondent covered the famous Dreyfus trial. He worked tirelessly for the foundation of a Jewish state, but died in 1904 at the age of 44, so never saw his dream realised.

In the grounds is a museum which details his life, and even has a replica of his study in Vienna with his own library and furniture.

The road past the museum leads to the tombs of Herzl and his family, the revisionist philosopher and spiritual leader of the Irgun Vladimir Jabotinsky, and Menahem Begin.

Other Israeli leaders who are buried here include Levy Eshkol and Golda Meir.

The path through the park ends at a cemetery for Jerusalem's fallen soldiers. The park is open daily 8am–6.45pm, and the museum Sun–Thurs 9am–6.45pm, Fri 9am–1pm, closed Saturday. There is no entrance fee. Take Bus 13, 17, 18, 20, 21 or 23.

Yad Vashem Memorial

Close to Mount Herzl is Har Ha Zikaron (Mount of Remembrance) dedicated to the six million Jews killed during World War II. The *Avenue of the Righteous Among the Nations* is a tree-lined boulevarde dedicated to non-Jews who helped save Jewish lives during the Holocaust, and it leads to the Yad Vashem Memorial.

The memorial is without doubt the most moving, and terrifying, of the museums of this era, and the incredible architecture has to be seen to be believed. The huge crypt-like stone room inside has a fire whose light casts an eerie glow over the plaques on the floor bearing the names Auschwitz, Dachau, etc.

In another building to the left there is a permanent exhibition of grizzly photographs and artifacts relating to the Nazi atrocities. There is also an art museum, and a *Hall of Names*, containing over 3 million pages of the names, photographs and details of those who perished.

There is also an enormous labyrinth dedicated to the *Destroyed Communities* in the valley below, and the incredible *Garden of the Children of the Holocaust* will reduce even the most cynical to tears. The complex is open Sun–Thurs 9am–5pm, Fri 9am–2pm. There is no entrance fee. Take Bus 13, 17, 18, 20, 21 or 23.

Ein Kerem

Between Mount Herzl and Hadassah Hospital, Ein Kerem is a picturesque, ancient village, which is believed to be the birthplace of John the Baptist. There is a Franciscan church in the centre of the village, built over the grotto where St John was born. The church is well worth a visit and has beautiful old paintings and tiles. An old spring in the village is called Mary's Well, and the *Church of the Visitation* on the opposite side of the village, is built on the site of Mary's visit to Elizabeth and Zachariah after the Annunciation.

There is a very interesting art gallery, Bet Mayan, in an old house next to Mary's Well. Take Bus 17.

Hadassah Medical Centre

Hadassah, the Women's Zionist Organisation of America, is responsible for the building of this $30 million complex, which includes a medical school, nursing school, hospital, dental and pharmacy schools and laboritories. The organisation also commissioned artist Marc Chagall to design the windows for its synagogue, and the result guaranteed 140,000 visitors a year would come to 'ooh' and 'ah' over the stained glass. There are twelve windows depicting the twelve tribes of Israel and they are incredibly beautiful.

Four of the windows were damaged in 1967, but two years later Marc Chagall replaced them. Incidentally, Mr Chagall donated the windows, and also the replacements.

The centre is open Sun–Thurs 8.30am–3.30pm, with guided tours on the hour. Take Bus 19 or 27.

Kennedy Memorial

About 8km (5 miles) from the Hadassah Medical Centre is Yad Kennedy, which was opened in May 1966. The 18m (60 ft) concrete memorial resembles a tree stump, symbolising John F. Kennedy, whose life was cut short by an assassin's bullet, and on a clear day can be seen from as far away as Tel Aviv. The concrete struts around the memorial each bear the seal of an American State. The interior is rather austere with an eternal flame, and a bust of the President.

Surrounding the hill is the Kennedy Peace Forest, which commemorates the former President and his brother, Robert

Kennedy, who was also tragically killed. Take Bus 20, and be prepared for a bit of a walk.

-The village to the west is Batir, site of the last Jewish revolt against the Romans by Bar Kochba in 135AD.

Tombs of the Sanhedrin

Also known as the Tombs of the Judges, these catacombs are much more finely carved than the Tombs of the Kings. The Sanhedrin was the high court and senate of the 1st and 2nd century, who ruled on grave legal matters, and would have reviewed the case against Jesus. The surrounding park is open Sun–Fri 9am–sunset, but the tombs are closed on Sunday. Take Bus 2 from the city centre.

Biblical Zoo

One of the most unusual collection of animals in the world, the Jerusalem Biblical Zoo is in the district of Romema. Prof Aaron Shulov of the Hebrew University has amassed all the plants, animals and birds mentioned in the Bible, even those that are not now indigenous to Israel. On the cage of each specimen is sign with an appropriate biblical passage. If you are travelling with children, a visit to the zoo is a must. Open 8am–sunset daily. There is an entrance fee, and tickets for Saturday must be bought in advance at either ticket agencies or at the zoo. Take Bus 15, 26 or 28.

Model of Ancient Jerusalem

The Holy Land Hotel, Harav Uziel Street, Bayit Vegan, ph 631 261, has a scaled-down model (1:50) in its gardens, of Jerusalem of the Second Temple Period, with its opulent palaces, giant walls and towers. The model took years to build by a team of architects, archeologists, historians and builders under the supervision of Prof M. Avi-Yonah. Open Sun–Thurs 8.30am–3.30pm, with tours on the half hour. Admission is 5.00NIS. Take Bus 21.

Islamic Art Museum

The L.A. Mayer Institute for Islamic Art, 2 HaPalmah Street, has a very good, chronologically displayed collection of miniatures, paintings and artifacts from the world of Islam. This is another interesting place that will keep children entertained. Open Sun–Thurs 10am–5pm, Sat 10am–1pm, closed Fri. Admission 6.00NIS, 4.50NIS Student. Take Bus 15.

NOTE: Bus 99 Circular Line travels to most places of interest. It departs at 10am, noon, 2pm, 4pm from Jaffa Gate, Sun–Thurs. Friday last service is 2pm. Also the last bus of the day does not stop at Yad Vashem. The cost is 3.10NIS.

TOURS

There are many tour companies offering tours in and around Jerusalem, and the Tourist Information Office is the best place to pick up details and schedules. Those we have listed below are by Galilee Tours whose office in Jerusalem is near the Central Bus Station, ph 383 460, and will give you an idea of what is available.

LOCAL TOURS
Tour 101 — Half-day — departing 9am Sun, Mon, Wed, 1.45pm Fri.
A three-hour walking tour of the Old City. Includes the Citadel, 15 minutes at the Western Wall, the Temple Mount, the Stations of the Cross and Church of the Holy Sepulchre — US$16.

Tour 102 — Half-day — departing 9am Tues, Thurs.
Travel to Mt Scopus and Mt of Olives, Garden of Gethsemane, Church of All Nations, Mary's Tomb, Garden Tomb, then on to Bethany, Home of Mary, Martha and Lazarus — US$18.

Tour 104 — Half-day — departing 9am Fri, 1.45pm Mon, Tues, Wed, Sat.
Visit Rachel's Tomb in Bethlehem, via the Church of the Nativity. Travel along the Hinnom Valley to Mt Zion to Tomb of King David, Chamber of the Holocaust and Room of the Last Supper. (Note: Rachel's Tomb is closed on Saturday and Jewish holidays.) — US$17.

Tour 105 — Half-day — departing 1.45pm Sun, Thurs.
Visit the Knesset (passport required), then drive through the New City to the Model of Jerusalem, then on to Yad Vashem — US$20.

Tour 120 — Full day — departing 9am Sun, Thurs. Combines Tours 101 and 105 — US$33.

Tour 122 — Full day — departing 9am daily except Sun, Thurs. Tour 101 plus visit to Mt Zion and Tomb of King David,

Dormition Abbey and Room of the Last Supper, then on to Rachel's Tomb (except on Saturday and Jewish holidays) and the Church of the Nativity — US$31.

TOURS FURTHER AFIELD

Tour 130 — Full day — departing 9am Sun, Tues, Fri.
Travel via the Judean Desert to Masada, on to Ein Gedi for visit to nature reserve/desert oasis, and swim in the Dead Sea — US$44.

Tour 131 — Full day — departing 9am Mon, Wed, Sat.
Via Judean Desert to Masada, continue along Dead Sea shore and stop for a swim, then on to Jericho — US$44.

Tour 140 — Full day — departing 7.30am Mon, Thurs, Fri, Sat.
Travel along coastal plain to Nazareth and visit Church of the Annunciation and St Joseph's Workshop. On to Capernium and the ancient synagogue and St Peter's house. Drive to the summit of the Mount of the Beatitudes, then back to the Sea of Galilee for a swim. Optional cruise on the Sea of Galilee if weather and time permit. Return via "Yardenit" on the Jordan River, with a possible visit to Netanya Diamond Centre — US$38.

Tour 143 — Full day — departing 7am Tues.
Drive across the Jordan River to Mitzpeh Gadot for a view of the Hula Valley. On to Qatzrin, visit the pool of Birkat Ram, then on to the springs of the Banias — US$42.

Tour 153 — Full day — departing 7am Wed.
Drive to Safed to see the ancient synagogue and artists' quarter. On to Meron to the Holy Tomb of Rabbi Simon Bar-Yochai. Then to Acre to the Crusader Knights' Hall and the old port. Ascend Mt Carmel for a view of Haifa Bay and the Baha'i Shrine —US$42.

Tour 158 — Full day — departing 7.30am Mon, Sat.
Travel the coastal plain via Mt Carmel to Haifa, visit Baha'i Shrine and gardens. On to Acre and Crusader Knights' Hall and port. Visit Caesarea on return trip — US$42.

Tour 161 — 2 days — departing 7.30am Mon.
First day — travel north to Nazareth, Church of the Annunciation and Joseph's Workshop. On to Tiberias, the Sea of Galilee, Capernium, Mount of Beatitudes. Overnight in Tiberias.

Second day — drive to the Golan Heights and the lookout of Mitzpeh Gadot. On to Qatzrin and Birkat Ram. Descend to the Banias, one of the sources of the Jordan River — 4-star hotel half-board US$140.

Tour 163 — 2 days — departing 7am Tues.
First day — drive to the Golan Heights and the Mitzpeh Gadot. On to Qatzrin and Birkat Ram. Descend to the Banias, then overnight in the Galilee.
Second day — Visit Safed, then drive to Meron and the Holy Tomb of Rabbi Simon Bar-Yochai. On to Acre, then ascend Mt Carmel before returning to Jerusalem — 4-star hotel half-board US$140.

Tour 165 — 3 days — departing 7.30am Monday.
First day — travel north to Nazareth and Church of the Annunciation and Joseph's Workshop. On to Tiberias, the Sea of Galilee, Capernium and Mount of Beatitudes. Overnight in the Galilee.
Second day — drive to the Golan Heights and the Mitzpeh Gadot, then on the Quatzrin and Birkat Ram, descend to Banias. Overnight in the Galilee.
Third day — visit Safed, the ancient synagogue and artists' quarter, then on to Meron and the Tomb of Rabbi Simon Bar-Yochai. Next stop Acre to visit the Knights' Hall and the old port. Ascend Mt Carmel for view of Haifa Bay — 4-star hotel half-board US$200.

SPORT AND RECREATION

Swimming
YMCA (West), King David Street — for members and guests — is open all year round — Bus 6, 15, 16.
   Jerusalem Public Pool, 43 Emek Refaim Street, ph 632 042 — Bus 4, 18.
      Bet Tailor, Zangwil Street, Kiryat Yovel, ph 414 362 — Bus 18.
      Kibbutz Ramat Rachel, ph 715 711 — Bus 7.
   There are pools at the hotels King David, Holy Land, Diplomat and President.

Tennis
Bet Tailor, ph 414 362; Holy Land Hotel, 661 101; Ramat Rachel, ph 715 711; YMCA (West), ph 227 111; Jerusalem Sports Club, 30 Hatzafira Street; German Colony, ph 632 125.

THE DEAD SEA

The Dead Sea is 396m (1300 ft) below sea level, the lowest point on the earth's surface. The sea is 'dead' because it contains no form of life due to its high salt concentration, which is eight times that of the Mediterranean Sea, the Atlantic Ocean or the Pacific Ocean. There are also high concentrations of magnesium, iodine and bromine, in fact ten to twenty times higher than in ocean water.

The level of the Sea is dropping slowly because the evaporation is quicker than the influx of water from the Jordan River. It is possible to see on the hills by the roadside the marks of former levels, and unless something is done, such as one plan for a canal to carry water from the Mediterranean, it will eventually disappear.

The evaporation also means that there is a constant cloud of haze over the sea, giving it a dreamy sort of atmosphere. People will say that it is impossible to get sunburnt near the sea, but I don't think there are any guarantees, and I wouldn't chance it.

Swimming in the Dead Sea is a unique experience. The high salinity enables you to float like a cork, and in fact you can't really do anything else. It is impossible to tread water, or kick, as your legs will just keep floating to the top, and as it is inadvisable to get the water in your eyes due to stinging you can't attempt to swim in the conventional manner — a great place for non-swimmers. As the water will let you know about any small scratches or cuts you may have, it is best to take your dip at one of the resorts, such as Ein Gedi, Ein Feshka, Ein Boqeq or Ne've Sohar, as they have fresh water showers available near the water's edge. Even so, it is best not to shave the day you are going to the Dead Sea.

Some scientists believe that the water may help in cases of skin allergies and glandular malfunctions, but it is not good for your hair, which explains why you will see so many people laying back with their necks at an acute angle, even if they're not reading a newspaper (which is the almost obligatory pose for snapshots).

Several resorts along the coast have sulphur springs, and these have been found to be of great benefit to sufferers of arthritis and rheumatism, but they can be harmful to people with high blood

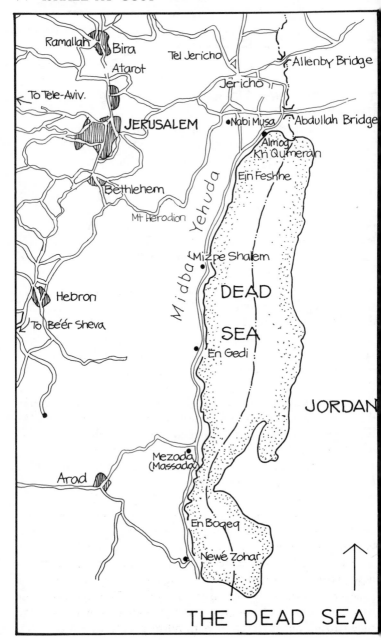

THE DEAD SEA

pressure, and there are warning signs to this effect. Some resorts even have a doctor on call to check blood pressure if anyone is in doubt. Even so, it is a case of all care but no responsibility.

This area is part of the West Bank, however as the attractions are not far from Jerusalem, we have decided to give it a section of its own.

BETHANY

The town of Bethany, on the western slope of the Mount of Olives, is mentioned many times in the Bible. It was here that Lazarus and his sisters Mary and Martha lived, and where Christ raised Lazarus from the dead (John 11:17–44). It was in Bethany that Christ cursed the fig tree (Mark 11:12–14) and Simon the leper lived when Christ visited and the woman (some believe it was Mary Magdalene) poured a flask of oil on His head (Mark 14:3–9).

HOW TO GET THERE

By Bus
Take city bus no. 43 from Jerusalem's municipal bus depot on Nablus Road (one block up from Damascus Gate).

By Car
Bethany is 4km (2 miles) from Jerusalem on the Jericho Road.

By Sherut
Hire from the Damascus Gate taxi stand.

SIGHTSEEING

Franciscan Church
The present church on the site where Lazarus lived was built in 1954 and features several interesting mosaics. There have been three other churches on the site, the first built in the 4th century BC, the second in the Byzantine period and the third by the Crusaders in the 2nd century AD.

The tower to the south of the church is part of the ruins of an abbey built by Queen Melisends, wife of Fulk of Anjou, the Crusader King of Jerusalem (1131–1143).

Tomb of Lazarus
The grotto in which Lazarus was interred is still there, and there is a flight of steps leading to it from the right-hand side of the church. (open 8am–noon, 2–6pm).

The Crusaders were certainly busy in this area. They built a church over the tomb, a monastery over Martha and Mary's house, and a tower over Simon's house.

Then, in the 16th century, the Muslims erected a mosque over the grotto. Above the tomb now is a small Greek Orthodox Church, but it's not generally open to the public.

A short walk along the main road leads to the Greek Orthodox Convent, which has a rock which they say Christ sat on while waiting for Martha to arrive from Jericho. (That one is a bit hard to believe.)

BETHANY TO THE DEAD SEA

As the Jericho Road continues on to its final destination, it passes through several Bedouin settlements, with people living in much the same way as they did in the days of Christ. While it is fascinating to see the young children tending the goats and sheep, and to note the living conditions, it is not advisable to stop and take a photograph. Some Bedouins may not mind, but others will.

Inn of the Good Samaritan
15km (9 miles) from Jerusalem is an outcrop of red rock known as the Ascent of Adummim, a border-marker between the tribes of Judah (Joshua 15:7). On the hill now stands the ruins of a Crusader castle.

As the crossroads here were an obvious spot for an overnight stop for travellers between Jerusalem and Jericho, this has always been an important part of the road. It was part of an ancient caravan route, and remains have been found of a Roman road.

On the road to the right from the Jericho Road is an old Turkish inn known as the Inn of the Good Samaritan, for it is believed that it is built on the spot mentioned in the parable (Luke 10:25–37).

Wadi Qelt
There are signposts on the main road pointing left to the Old Jericho Road and the Greek Orthodox Monastery of St George, which is built near a spring named Wadi Kelt. Enthusiastic hikers

will revel in the Wadi Qelt gorge, which is an oasis in the Judean Desert, and the trek from the turnoff to Jericho takes about four hours. For centuries people have used the water of the spring, building aqueducts to carry it away, and even today it is used to irrigate part of Jericho.

The Monastery of St George overlooking the gorge, is built into the side of a cliff. It was once a busy settlement of thousands of monks but today there are only a handful who lead a simple life of prayer. Visitors are allowed, but modest dress is a necessity.

Returning to the main road (Route 1) there is a cairn marking Sea Level, and soon the Dead Sea comes into view.

Nebi Musa (Tomb of Moses)
On the right side of the road in the distance is a Muslim shrine, marking what they believe to be the grave of Moses. The Old Testament says that Moses died in the Land of Moab, but no one knows where he was buried (Deut. 34:5–6). The Arabs believe that Allah brought the body from its secret grave to this site.

Not far from here there is a road branching off to the left which leads to Jericho, but for the Dead Sea continue east and then take the big sweep to the right. Let's take the road to the left first.

JERICHO

The Book of Joshua (2–6) tells the story of his Battle of Jericho with the help of Rahab, the prostitute, but as mentioned in the first section on the history of Israel, the latter-day excavations have not revealed the existence of a wall at that period of time. What they have found is that there have been 23 cities built on the site, the earliest in the 8th millenium BC, backing up Jericho's claim to being the oldest city in the world.

Why was the spot so popular that so many different civilisations decided to build their cities here? Well water was one of the main reasons, particularly as the surrounding region is so dry and barren. The nearby Spring of Elisha, also known as Sultan's Spring, is the one which the Bible says Elisha sweetened (2 Kings 2:19–22), and is still responsible for making Jericho such an eternally coveted oasis — although it now has a pump-house.

The hills behind Jericho are thought to be the wilderness where Christ was tempted by Satan (Luke 4:1–13). Anyone who spends a few hours out in the sun in this part of the world will understand what Christ must have suffered in those 40 days, even without Satan.

HOW TO GET THERE

By Bus
Take Bus 961 or 963 from the Central Bus Station in Jerusalem.

By Car
Jericho is 39km (24 miles) east of Jerusalem.

SIGHTSEEING

The archaeological site of Jericho is called Tel es-Sultan, and has access roads, a car park filled with locals hawking their wares plus a few camels, toilet facilities, and one covered observation platform. The site is well-signposted with dates of the digs and the names of the people in charge of them. There are the remains of what looks to be a dam, which is interesting considering there is no river, but maybe they had problems with water draining from the hills.

It's one of those places where you really have to use your imagination, as the tel is distinctly unimpressive. Open daily 8am–5pm, admission 4NIS adult, 2NIS children.

From the observation platform you can see the Ein El Sultan Refugee Camp, which was one of the largest camps on the West Bank, but most of its inhabitants fled across the Jordan River during the Six Day War.

Across the street is Elisha's Spring, and the water is still drinkable.

On the mountains to the west is a Greek Orthodox monastery, built on what is thought to be the Mount of Temptation. In the monastery is a rock with an inscription saying (in Greek) that this was where Christ was tempted by the devil and served by angels.

North of the tel are signs leading to Hisham's Palace, an enormous place built by the Umayyads in the 8th century. Apparently it was for the caliphs from Damascus to holiday in the winter, but it was destroyed by earthquake before they experienced its delights. You shouldn't miss the mosaic of the Tree of Life in the bathhouse.

Between New Jericho and Old Jericho there are quite a few garden restaurants lining the sides of the road where you can get a reasonably-priced lunch. Obviously the more crowded the establishment, the better the food. The Mount of Temptation Restaurant next to the ancient city has good salads, and of course, felafels.

Now back to the main road, continue east, then take the big sweep to the right.

QUMRAN

On the north-western shore of the Dead Sea is Qumran, known to the Arabs as Khirbet Qumran. It was here in 1947 that the Dead Sea Scrolls were found, quite by accident. Muhammad Adh-Dhib, a Bedouin shepherd was looking for a lost member of his flock and presumed that it had gone into one of the caves in the cliffs. He threw a stone in the cave to frighten the animal, and the stone hit something that made him investigate further. Inside he found several earthernware jars containing what he thought were scraps of old leather. He took some pieces to a cobbler in Bethlehem and sold them. The shopkeeper showed them to the local Assyrian Orthodox Bishop, who thought they could be ancient manuscripts and bought them for about US$250. He showed them to Prof Sukenk, a Hebrew scholar, who agreed and consulted a Dr Trever, who identified one as a copy of the Book of Daniel. Evidence has since revealed that they were written about 100BC.

Subsequently scrolls were found in eleven caves and they contained parts of every book of the old testament, verifying the modern versions.

The scrolls were apparently written by a Jewish sect, the Essenes, who lived a communal life nearby. Excavations on the site of their commune began in 1951, and the entire complex has now been uncovered. According to the sign at the site of the excavations: "The sect's main principle of faith was a strict adherence to Mosaic Law and belief in predestination, according to which all creatures were divided into the Sons of Light and the Sons of Darkness, destined to struggle at the end of days, in heaven and on earth, until the Sons of Light should prevail. The members of the sect rejected the temple priesthood, established

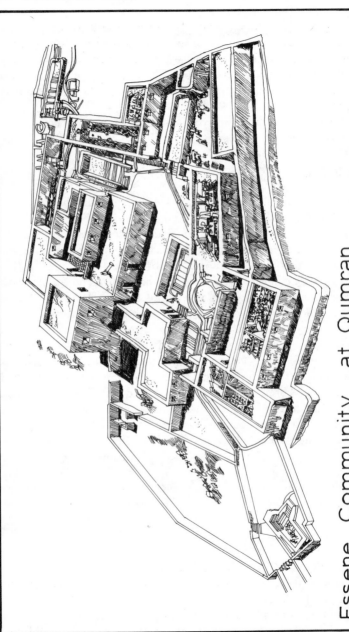

Essene   Community   at   Qumran

their own solar calendar and set forth stringent laws of purity and impurity. In order to carry out all their religious precepts, they settled in the desert, founding a community based on their beliefs, in preparation for the end of days."

There are some who claim that John the Baptist may have been a member of this sect.

HOW TO GET THERE

By Bus
From Jerusalem Bus 486, 487, 421 or 966 pass by the turnoff to Qumran.

By Car
Qumran is 43km (27 miles) south-east of Jerusalem, and the excavations are 400m from the highway.

SIGHTSEEING

If you have forgotten your hat, or water, drop into the small cafeteria-cum-souvenir shop first, because you'll need both. It doesn't take much energy to view the archaeological site, but there's no shade, except further along when you go to gaze across at Cave No. IV where the first scrolls were found, but it's very hot, barren country, so be warned. And if you wish to actually climb up to inspect the cave at close quarters, which is only recommended for the extremely fit, take litres of water.

The ruins of the commune are well sign-posted in English and Hebrew, but it is best to start your explorations by climbing to the top of the watchtower which overlooks the site, to get your bearings.

There is a cluster of buildings grouped around a canal system, specially designed for the baptism rituals of the Essenes. Clearly visible are the aqueduct, the bathing pool and the seven major cisterns which carried the water to other pools and several of the buildings. The community was completely self-sufficient, having a mill and bakery in this complex, and a farm about 2km to the south. Of particular interest are the scriptorium, where the scrolls were probably written, and the pottery where the jars they were kept in were made.

The site is open Sun–Thurs 8am–5pm, Fri 8am–4pm, and there is an admission fee.

EIN-GEDI

Ein-Gedi is a large oasis, with an abundance of plant and animal life, due to the many fresh-water springs. Rain falling in the Judean Mountains permeates the ground and trickles through the rock strata. Most of the water flows along two wadi beds bordering the oasis, Nahal David in the north, and Nahal Arugot in the south, but some of it emerges on the slopes in the form of smaller springs, such as Ein-Gedi Spring and Shulamit Spring (nahal = brook)

Ein-Gedi is mentioned twice in the Bible. David hid here to escape the wrath of Saul (1 Sam. 23:29,24:1), and in the Song of Songs it is referred to as the "Fountain of the Kid", which it is still sometimes called.

Its history goes back to the Calcolithic Age, around 3000BC, and there are ruins of a temple from this era. There were settlements here in the Persian, Hellenistic, Roman, Byzantine and early Muslim periods. Mostly they were agricultural communities that cultivated plants for medical and cosmetic use. At the mouth of the Nahal David, about 100m to the right of the car park some ancient wooden coffins and a large number of skeletons were found in caves.

There are traces of ancient aqueducts and pools on the slopes below the Ein-Gedi Spring.

HOW TO GET THERE

By Bus

From the Central Bus Station in Jerusalem take Bus 421, 486, 487 or 966. When leaving the bus follow the signs to Nahal David, not Ein-Gedi, which will take you to the kibbutz of the same name.

By Car

Ein-Gedi is 163km (101 miles) from Jerusalem, and 34km (21 miles) from Qumran.

ACCOMMODATION

The kibbutz has a guest house, ph 057 90874, and there are trailers for rent at the Ein-Gedi Camping Village.

SIGHTSEEING

At Ein-Gedi there is an unusual combination of water plants and desert plants, and at least twelve species of native trees, some of which are only found here. Make sure you check out the Apple of Sodom tree just outside the entrance gate.

There are herds of ibex roaming free and everyone says there are leopards in the park, but I'll bet you don't see one.

The Nature Reserve is honey-combed with hiking trails — some short, and some more extended:

1. Along Nahal David, to the waterfall and the pools — about 1.5 hours.

2. To Ein-Gedi Spring, the Calcolithic Temple and Dodim Cave — about 4 hours.

3. Via Ein-Gedi Spring and the Calcolithic Temple to the Dry Waterfall — about 5 hours.

4. Via Ein-Gedi Spring to the Ein-Gedi Observation Post, and back — about 7 hours.

5. Along Nahal Arugot to the Hidden Waterfall — about 4 hours.

6. To the Har-Ishai Observation Point and Nahal David — about 5 hours.

Detailed information on the hiking trails can be obtained at the Ein-Gedi Field School in the Reserve, or from the Wardens.

About 5km (3 miles) south of the Reserve is the Ein-Gedi Spa, a modern complex on the shores of the Dead Sea. It has hot sulphur baths (segregated), excellent changing facilities with free lockers, a snack bar, an inexpensive restaurant, and a free bus to take you the 100 odd metres to the swimming area in the Dead Sea.

The complex is run by the Ein-Gedi Kibbutz, and they also manufacture a range of skin-care products, which have as their base the famous Dead Sea black mud. Before you buy you can have a test run near the swimming area with the real thing. The idea is that you plaster the mud all over, leave it on until it sets, then shower it off at the open-air showers near the sea, and presto! — you look 10 years younger. Anyway, it's a lot of fun, but the mud is quite difficult to rinse off.

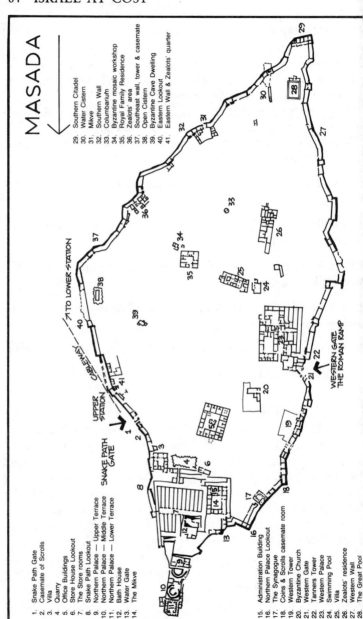

MASADA

1. Snake Path Gate
2. Casemate of Scrolls
3. Villa
4. Quarry
5. Office Buildings
6. Store House Lookout
7. The Store rooms
8. Snake Path Lookout
9. Northern Palace — Upper Terrace
10. Northern Palace — Middle Terrace
11. Northern Palace — Lower Terrace
12. Bath House
13. Water Gate
14. The Mikve

15. Administration Building
16. Northern Palace Lookout
17. The Synagogue
18. Coins & Scrolls casemate room
19. Western Tower
20. Byzantine Church
21. Western Gate
22. Tanners Tower
23. Western Palace
24. Swimming Pool
25. Villa
26. Zealots' residence
27. Western Wall
28. The Great Pool

29. Southern Citadel
30. Water Cistern
31. Mikve
32. Southern Wall
33. Columbarium
34. Byzantine mosaic workshop
35. Royal Family Residence
36. Zealots' area
37. Southeast wall, tower & casemate
38. Open Cistern
39. Byzantine Cave Dwelling
40. Eastern Lookout
41. Eastern Wall & Zealots' quarter

MASADA

Masada, the stronghold, is an isolated plateau, rising 427m (1400 ft) above the Dead Sea shore. It was first fortified by the Maccabean king Alexander Jannaeus (103-76BC) but the only things that have been found from this period are coins.

In 40BC Herod, then an influential nobleman, became involved in a local civil war between pro-Parthian and pro-Roman factions. Herod supported Rome, so he had to make himself scarce because the Parthian-appointed King was after him. So he dumped his family and his private army on top of Masada and took off for Rome. There he was nominated by the Senate as King of Judea, and he returned in 37BC with two Roman legions to claim his crown.

Terrified of an open revolt, and petrified that Cleopatra would finally talk Marc Antony into giving her Judea, Herod built a royal sanctuary and fortress on Masada's summit. When he died in 4BC, the whole kit and caboodle passed to his son, Archelaus, who was no match for the Romans and they took control.

In 66AD the Jews revolted against Rome and the garrison at Masada was overpowered by zealots under the leadership of Ben-Yehuda the Galilean. This gave the Jews an armed camp within easy striking distance of the Roman forces in the interior.

Jerusalem fell in 70AD, and any survivors fled to Masada bolstering the forces there, and enabling it to hold out against the Romans for three years until the arrival of the Tenth Roman Legion under the command of Flavius Silva. He realised that a siege would not work, so he decided to have a ramp built up to the lowest point of the plateau and attack with a mobile siege tower equipped with catapults, arrow launchers and a giant battering ram. It worked.

Josephus, in *The Jewish War*, writes of the moving speech made by the Jewish leader Eleazar, suggesting that it would be better to commit suicide than be captured and taken into slavery. It is a remarkable speech, especially considering that Josephus was not there, and the two women and five little children who he said were the only ones to survive, could not possibly have remembered such a long speech verbatim. Anyway, Eleazar obviously said something for indeed the Jews did suicide rather than be taken, all, again according to Josephus, "nine hundred and sixty, women and children included". The Romans occupied the site only for a short time before abandoning it. Then in the fifth century a group of Byzantine monks took up residence, living in caves and amongst the rubble, but they didn't stay for long.

Masada was deserted until 1963 when the archeologists moved in, headed by Yigal Yadin of the Hebrew University of Jerusalem. The volunteers from Israel and other parts of the world made their camp on the Roman ramp and worked throughout the winter months of 1963 and 1964.

In 1970 the cableway was completed, providing an easier approach for visitors. The cars rise over 305m (1000 ft) from the base on the eastern side to a terminus some 18m (60 ft) beneath the summit.

HOW TO GET THERE
By Bus
The same buses that stop at Ein-Gedi go on to Masada.
By Car
Masada is 20km (12 miles) south of Ein-Gedi, a few kilometres inland on the road to Beersheva.

How to get up to the Site
A cable car leaves every 15 minutes from the station near the cafeteria and souvenir shop. The first trip is at 8am and the last is at 4pm (2pm on Friday).

There are two walking trails to the stop — the Roman Ramp, which is the easiest, and the original Snake Path, which the zealots used, and which has not really been altered. It's not hard to see why it is called the Snake Path, as it twists its way up, and the walk takes just under an hour. Don't attempt it in the middle of the day.

SIGHTSEEING
Toilet facilities, drinking fountains and sun shelters have been erected on the site, which is about 610m (2000 ft) from north to south, and 198m (650 ft) from east to west, but it is imperative that you take plenty of water, and wear a hat.

There are about 40 points of interest, so be prepared to spend a few hours, and taking a snack is a good idea. Some of the most interesting are:

The *Store Houses* — Overlooking the eastern cliffside, Herod had a large complex of rectangular storehouses erected. Each apparently contained one type of foodstuff. Excavations have proved that it was possible for an army to withstand a long siege without outside supplies.

The *Northern Palace* — Built as Herod's palatial residence in three tiers, it is on the highest point of Masada. Of interest is a hidden staircase connecting the three terraces, but invisible from the outside. There's no doubt Herod liked his privacy. He was also a tricky devil. The western interior pillar line has plaster panelling, painted to look like marble. The colours are still preserved, and have now been covered with plastic to protect from vandalism. Also the lower terrace has columns which Josephus described as being "carved out of a single stone", but now that the plaster covering has gone it is easy to see that they were made out of fitted stone drums, then covered with plaster and grooved to make them appear monolithic.

The *Synagogue* — Thought to be the oldest synagogue yet discovered in Israel, it baffled the archeologists as to its purpose until they found beneath its floor two scrolls of Deuteronomy and Ezekiel, which had been buried by the zealots, as is still the custom today.

The *Byzantine Church* — A small chapel built by the monks who lived here in the fifth century.

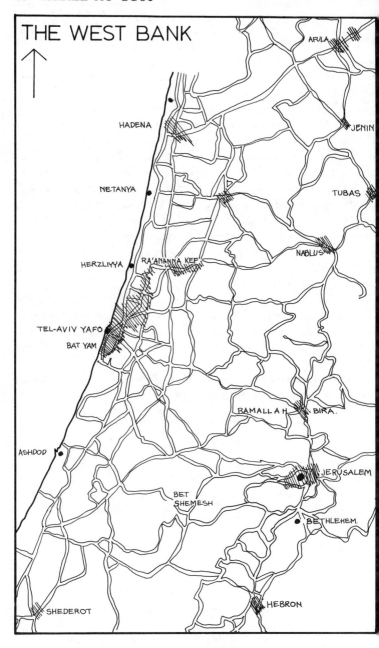

THE WEST BANK

THE WEST BANK

The West Bank has been under Israeli control since the Six Day War of 1967, and they prefer to call it Judea and Samaria. Judea is the region south of Jerusalem and includes Bethlehem and Hebron. Samaria is north of Jerusalem, and its largest city is Nablus, the Biblical Shechem.

The area is really in a political mess, but as visitors it is really none of our business. Suffice to say that travellers are unlikely to come across any open hostility, and if they stick to the main routes they are going to be perfectly safe.

It is obvious wherever you go in Israel that there is no love lost between the two races involved, but if you have picked up a bit of Hebrew on your travels, this is not the place to practise it. In fact if you are in an Arab district, and most of the people living on the West Bank are Arab, it is better to deny any knowledge of Hebrew at all, and in any case many Palestinians speak English.

The Jewish holidays and the Shabbat are not observed on the West Bank, but during the holy month of Ramadan many of the restaurants will be closed until sundown.

JUDEA

BETHLEHEM

One of the most sacred places on the West Bank, Bethlehem is a pretty little town, which features prominently in the Biblical record. It was here that Rachel died giving birth to Benjamin (Genesis 35:16–20), Ruth met and married Boaz (Ruth 1:22–4:10), David was born and later anointed King of Israel (1 Samuel 16) and Jesus Christ was born (Luke 2:1–7).

It was in a cave in this area, in the 4th century, that St Jerome translated the Hebrew Bible into Latin. This translation is known as the Vulgate, and is still the accepted translation for the Roman Catholic Church.

HOW TO GET THERE

By Bus
Take Bus 34 or 44 from the Nablus Road bus depot in Jerusalem.

By Car
Bethlehem is 10km (6 miles) from Jerusalem.

ACCOMMODATION

As Bethlehem is so close to Jerusalem, it is best to make a day trip. But if you are determined to spend a night in this holy town, here are some names and addresses with prices in US Dollars for a double room, including breakfast. The Telephone Area Code is 02.

Paradise, Manger Street, ph 744 542 — $40; Bethlehem Star, Al Baten Street, ph 743 249 — $35; Grand Bethlehem, Paul 6th Street, ph 741 440 — $35.

EATING OUT

Granada Grill Bar, New Tourists Shopping Centre, ph 742 810 — Middle Eastern — under 20NIS.

El Andalus Restaurant, Manger Square, ph 743 519 — local food — 20–40NIS.

Vienna Restaurant, Milk Grotto Street, ph 742 783 — European — 20–40NIS.

St George Restaurant, next to Tourist Information Office, ph 743 780 — al fresco — under 20NIS.

SIGHTSEEING

Rachel's Tomb
The present tomb was built by Moses Montefiore in 1860, but there have been several synagogues on the site throughout history. Rachel, the wife of Jacob and mother of Joseph, is venerated by Muslims, Jews and Christians, but the majority of pilgrims here are women praying for fertility — which seems a little odd as Rachel died in childbirth. Anyway, the building is not very impressive. It is open Sun–Thurs 8am–5pm, Fri 8am–1pm, and is at the northern end of town at the junction of Manger Street and Hebron Road.

Church of the Nativity
The first church on the site of the birth of Christ was built in 326 by Constantine (at his mother Helena's urging). The present

fortress, sorry, church resulted from rebuilding by Justinian in the 6th century, and repairs by the Crusaders in the 12th century. At the front of the church are the square doorway of Justinian and the arched doorway of the Crusaders, but they were both blocked up during medieval times, as were the windows, as a safety precaution. The present opening, called the Door of Humility, necessitates bending over to walk through, the idea being that Muslims couldn't enter on horseback. Incidentally, Orthodox Jews won't enter either because by bending over they would be bowing their heads in a Christian church.

The inside of the church is a bit of a disappointment, although there is evidence that the previous churches may have been more befitting. There are huge wooden trapdoors in the centre of the marble Crusader floor which open up to show the beautiful mosaic floor of Constantine's church. Four rows of reddish limestone Corinthian columns, and mosaic fragments along the walls are all that remain from Justinian's. The icons decorating the altar were presented in 1764 by the Russian royal family, and the English Oak ceiling was a gift from the English king Edward IV. The Greek Orthodox Church runs the basilica, but other services are held here on a roster system.

The Grotto of the Nativity, the place where Christ was actually born, is reached by stairs on either side of the high altar in the church. They descend to a cave, which is quite smoke-stained from all the candles, where there is a large silver star marking the spot. A couple of metres away is the Chapel of the Manager, where Mary placed the newborn babe. (One thing should be mentioned here. A lot of people are under the impression that the manger was the place where Christ was born. In fact a manger is a feed-trough for animals, probably from the French manger = to eat). St Luke says Mary "wrapped him in swaddling cloths, and laid him in a manger, because there was no room for them in the inn" (Luke 2:7). The fact that there was a manger in close proximity indicates that they were in a stable, but it must be remembered that in those days it was quite common to keep livestock in a cave.

St Catherine's Church

Adjacent to the Church of the Nativity, and linked by a door in the many body of the church, is the Roman Catholic church, St

Catherine's. It is light, bright and quite beautiful, in stark contrast to the church next door. It is here that the traditional Midnight Mass is celebrated on Christmas Eve.

There are also a few grottoes under this church. One has the Chapel of St Joseph, where the angel commanded him to take his family and flee to Egypt (Matthew 2:13), and another has the Chapel of the Innocents, recalling the babies killed by Herod (Matthew 2:16). A third contains the Chapel of St Jerome as this is where he translated the scriptures, but his remains are now in Rome.

Manger Square
The square outside the Church of the Nativity is always a hive of activity, but it really comes alive at Christmas, and it has three. First there is the Western Christmas Eve on December 24, then the Greek Orthodox celebrations on January 7, and the Armenian on January 19. Each has a colourful procession with which the patriarch of the respective church journeys from Jerusalem.

The Western Christmas celebrations continue on into the evening and culminate with the Midnight Mass, which is televised on a giant screen in the Square for the people unable to get into the church.

Milk Grotto
On Milk Grotto Street, which runs off Manger Square is the Milk Grotto. The Holy Family hid here before fleeing to Egypt, and according to tradition, the nursing Mary dropped some of her milk onto the rocks which immediately turned chalky white. Whether you want to believe this or not, little packets of the powdered white stone are sold here and are said to increase the milk flow of nursing mothers. The church is open daily 8–11.45am, 2–5pm.

Kind David's Well
About 50m north of Manger Square are three restored cisterns of Kind David's Well in the car park of the King David Cinema. This is the well that David wanted water from when Bethlehem was in the control of the Philistines (2 Samuel 23:14–16). The cinema presents a 2-hour movie called *Jesus* at 10.30am, 2pm, 5pm and 8.30pm. The movie was made in Israel under the supervision of a team of historical and biblical scholars, and is quite well done.

Field of Ruth

About 4km east of Bethlehem on Route 356 is the Arab village of Beit Sahur and near here is the Field of Ruth, where it is believed her meeting with Boaz took place. Beit Sahur means 'House of the Shepherds', and there are two places here that vie for recognition as the place where the shepherds kept 'watch over their flock by night' (Luke 2:8). The Roman Catholic field, on the left fork of the road, is probably the most interesting, but to be fair, I suppose, you should also visit the Greek Orthodox field on the right fork.

Herodium

Built in the first century BC, the Herodium, as you probably guessed by the name, was another of the palace-fortresses of Herod the Great. This was also a stronghold of the Jewish zealots in the Jewish revolt against the Romans. It sits on top of a mountain that Herod had reshaped into an almost perfect cone with a flat top. He then built, in his usual flamboyant style, a palace with ritual baths, storerooms, a flight of marble steps winding down the mountainside, defensive walls and towers.

Josephus says in *The Jewish War* that Herod wished to be buried here, and was subsequently, but his tomb has never been found.

The Herodium is open daily 8am–5pm, 4pm of Friday.

HEBRON

A very ancient town, and identified in the Bible as the place were Sarah died and Abraham purchased the land to bury her from Ephron the Hittite (Genesis 23). In the Book of Numbers it is also recorded that Moses sent spies to Hebron to see what the land and the people were like. The spies brought back a bunch of grapes, and the Bible says "they carried it between two of them on a pole" (Numbers 13:23) — maybe a slight exaggeration, but Hebron is still known for the size and quality of its grapes. Incidentally this is where the Israel's Ministry of Tourism gets its symbol.

Unfortunately, this is not always a peaceful part of Israel, and it is often better to go on a guided tour than to travel independently.

HOW TO GET THERE

By Bus
Take Bus no. 34, 440 or 443 from the Central Bus Station in Jerusalem.

By Car
Hebron is 35km (22 miles) from Jerusalem on Route 60.

ACCOMMODATION

It is not recommended that you stay in Hebron, in fact it is advisable to leave before sunset.

SIGHTSEEING

Cave of Makhpelah
The four Holy Cities of Israel are Jerusalem, Tiberius, Safed and Hebron, and the Cave of Makhpelah containing the Tombs of the Patriarchs is what makes Hebron one of the holy four.

To Jews the sacred Tomb of the Patriarchs is second in importance only to the Wailing Wall in Jerusalem, but due to the continuing political situation, and the fact that the Arabs control the site, they have not always been able to visit the tomb. As the Bible tells that Abraham actually bought the land, it is one of three places in Israel that the Jews can really claim, in spite of who is in charge. The others are the Jerusalem Temple and the Tomb of Joseph.

The patriarchs, and matriarchs, buried here are Sarah, Abraham, Isaac, Jacob, Rebecca and Leah, but their remains are in a grotto well below the visible buildings. The surrounding fortress was built by Herod, of the same stones as the Western Wall in Jerusalem. A mosque was added in the 12th century, and until 1967 non-Muslims were forbidden entry. Now it is open Sat–Thurs 7.30–11.30am and 1.30–4pm. Muslims may enter between 11.30am–1.30pm, and they are the only ones who can visit on Friday and on Muslim holidays.

The main basilica is reminscent of the Dome of the Rock, with inlaid wood and ornate mosaics. Along the walls there are inscriptions from the Koran, and in the main section there are 'tombs' of Isaac and Rebecca. Those of Abraham and Sarah are in the adjoining courtyard, behind a silver grating, and opposite are those of Jacob and Leah.

Next door is a shrine to Joseph, which the Muslims believe is his tomb, but it is more generally accepted that the tomb at Nablus is the correct site.

Oak of Abraham

This is thought by some to be the biblical Mamre, which is mentioned a few times in the Book of Genesis, and then was the place were Abraham was told that Isaac would be born (Gen:18). Tradition also says that the Holy Family rested here on their way back from Egypt. The Russian Orthodox Church built a monastery around the oak tree in 1871, and visitors have been souveniring parts of it ever since the Middle Ages.

Of course, some have to disagree that this is the authentic tree (and how many trees live to be 3000 years old?), and even that this is the right place. They nominate Bet Ilanim, to the north of Hebron, where some Herodian walls, Roman temples and a 4th century Christian chapel have been excavated.

SAMARIA

Ramallah is the first town on the road north from Jerusalem, Route 60. On the way the road passes through Shu'afat, biblical Gibeah, the capital when Saul became the first King of Israel. Next comes a turn off to the Tomb of the Prophet Samuel, then on to Ramallah.

Ramallah was once the most popular summer resort in Jordan, but since its takeover by the Israelis naturally-enough it has lost its Arab clientele, and many of its facilities have closed down. Even the tourist office next to the bus station has been evacuated.

Nevertheless it is a very pretty town, and the area was the home of the Tribe of Benjamin.

Things to see include the large park with its children's playground, and the rather ornate former palace of King Hussein.

BETHEL

Situated about 5km (3 miles) north of Ramallah is the Arab village of Beitin — the biblical Bethal, which means "House of God". Genesis 12 has a couple of references to Bethel in regard to Abraham and Lot, and Genesis 28:10–19 tells of the Lord appearing to Jacob in a dream and of a ladder which "reached to heaven". This hill is called Jacob's Ladder, and although the site has been excavated quite extensively, there is nothing much to interest the visitor.

Further north is Shiloh, the place where the Ark of the Covenant rested after Joshua's conquest, but there's not much to see here either.

NABLUS

The largest city on the West Bank, Nablus is the biblical Shechem, although the ancient city is actually just south of the modern. It was at Shechem that Abraham first entered the land of Canaan (Genesis 12:6). Jacob came along, pitched his tent, and bought the land from the children of Hamor, Shechem's father (Genesis 33:18–20), making this another of the three places that belong to the Jews, in their opinion, by right of purchase. And it was at Shechem that Joseph was buried after the children of Israel brought his bones back from Egypt (Joshua 24:32).

HOW TO GET THERE

By Bus
Buses run from the Arab bus station on Nablus Road in Jerusalem, but the trip takes about 2.5 hours, and sherut taxis are quicker, more comfortable, and you may be able to arrange a good price.

By Car
Nablus is 63km (39 miles) from Jerusalem.

ACCOMMODATION
It is not really a tourist town, and not recommended as the safest place in the world to spend the night.

SIGHTSEEING

Mount Gerizim
Just south of Nablus, the Samaritans believe this to be Mount Sinai, and the site of Abraham's altar, on which he was prepared to sacrifice Isaac. (The most popular venue for this event is believed to be Mount Moriah in Jerusalem). The present Samaritans trace back their ancestry to the people who were left behind when the

Place of the birth of Jesus Christ, Church of the Nativity, Bethlehem

Headless red porphry Statue in Byzantine Street, Crusader City, Caesarea.

Babylonians captured the population of Israel in the 6th Century BC. When the Jews returned after being released by Cyrus, the Samaritans offered to help reconstruct the Temple, but the Jews refused their help, saying that the Samaritans were no longer Jews as they had intermarried with other races. The two factions were at loggerheads, and still are, to a certain extent, although early in this century the Samaritans decided to allow their young men to take Jewish brides.

The Samaritans claim that they are the only ones who have continuously inhabited Israel, and that they are the keepers of a Pentateuch, or Five Books of Moses, which was given to them by Aaron, Moses' brother. If the latter is true, it is the oldest biblical scroll in existence.

There are only about 600 Samaritans left today, about half of whom live in Nablus, closely resembling their Arab neighbours. The other half live in Holon, near Tel Aviv.

The Samaritans all gather on Mount Gerizim, at the site of Abraham's Altar, for the Passover sacrifice and slaughter a lamb, roast it and eat it quickly at midnight as ordered in the Book of Exodus.

Jacob's Well

The well is in the Greek Orthodox Covent of Jacob's Well. In the complex there are groups of immaculate gardens, a small station for prayer with a picture of Jesus and the Woman of the Well, the convent's other name. There are also two blue pillars, mounted with Roman capital stones that support a ceramic arch leading to the shrine and a huge unfinished church, which the Russian Orthodox church started in 1912, but stopped because of World War I. After the war all Russian Orthodox holy places in Israel were transferred to the Greek Orthodox church.

There is only one monk in charge of the complex now, but 80-odd years ago several monks were needed to help the hundreds of pilgrims who came, believing in the recuperative properties of the water.

The well is about 35m deep, and the original stones have been built on by the Mamelukes, Romans, Byzantines and Greeks, so the part from Jacob's time is at the very bottom.

The complex is open Mon–Sat 8am–noon, 2–5pm.

Joseph's Tomb

The traditional site of Joseph's Tomb is about a hundred metres north of Jacob's Well. The tomb was a Muslim shrine, and is very similar to Rachel's. It has now been taken over by the Israelis and is open daily 6am–6pm.

Sebastia/Samaria

Sebastia is the Roman name and Samaria the biblical name of the site that Omri, and his son Ahab, whose wife was Jezebel, made the capital of the northern Kingdom of Israel, after the death of Solomon, and did all sorts of things to upset the Lord (1 Kings 16:23–33). However the kingdom lasted for quite a long time, until it was destroyed by the Assyrians in 722 BC.

There are extensive remains of Ahab's Palace, but the more interesting parts are from the Roman and Herodian period, such as the amphitheatre, acropolis and the columned streets. The site is open Sat–Thurs 8am–5pm, Fri 9am–4pm.

In the nearby Arab village of Sebastiya is a mosque which was a Crusader Cathedral built over what was thought to be the burial place of John the Baptist. The mosque is called the Mosque of Nabi Yahya, the Arabic name for St John.

THE NEGEV AND SOUTH COAST

The Negev, which means 'dry land' makes up the southern half of Israel, and has its northern border approximately 27km (17 miles) north of Beersheba, the only large city in the region. Its eastern side is the Jordanian border and its western the Egyptian border.

Although primarily a desert with its fair share of sand, the Negev has mountains, canyons and a surprisingly wide variety of plant and animal life. It also has stretches of fertile fields, usually belonging to kibbutzes, which are the result of modern technology in bringing water from Lake Tiberias to irrigate the artificial oases.

The Negev Mountains, which border on the Sinai, have some of the most dramatic scenery in Israel, but they are almost uninhabited, and the only way to explore them is with a special-interest tour arranged by the Society for the Protection of Nature in Israel (enquire at the Tourist Information Office).

The history of the Negev is long and varied — the ancient Israelites, the Nabateans and the Romans all had fortifications here in their various eras, and the modern Israelis have many army bases, built after their withdrawal from the Sinai in 1982. But through all this has been the constant presence of the Bedouins, a race of nomadic people who originally roamed over the whole area, but have had their wanderings curtailed as more and more land is taken for agriculture. Some, under government pressure, have actually taken up permanent residence, and their 'villages' are easily recognisable, but others refuse to conform. Even those in the settlements give the impression of temporary habitation, which proves that you can take the boy out of the desert, but you can't take the desert out of the boy.

BEERSHEBA

When Israel took over the control of Beersheba from the Egyptians in 1948, it was a town of less than 2,000 people. It is now a modern city of about 130,000, with modern architecture, a university and all the accoutrements of the 20th century. If it

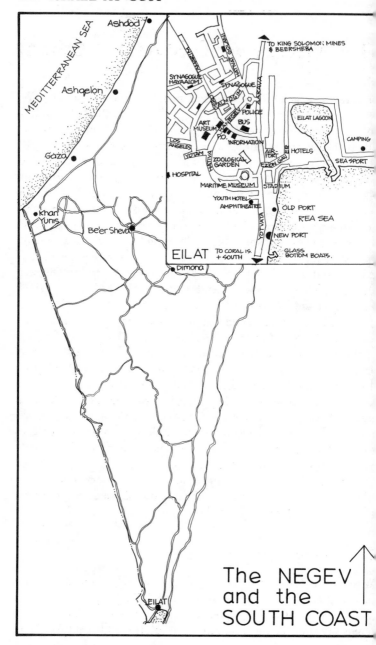

asn't for the camel caravans that still come into the town, you
ould believe that you had left Israel.

About 8km (5 miles) east of this modern city is the tel of the
ncient city of Beersheba, where Abraham made a covenant with
bimelech, king of Gerar. It seems Abimelech's servants took
ver a well which Abraham had dug, so to settle Abraham's
ntitlement to the well he gave Abimelech seven ewe lambs, and
ne two of them swore an oath (Genesis 21:25–32). Beersheba
neans 'well of seven' and 'well of the oath' in Hebrew.

Isaac's servants also dug a well here and Genesis 26:32–33
eports, "So he called it Shebah. Therefore the name of the city is
Beersheba to this day".

The Bible repeats many times the phrase "From Dan to
Beersheba", and this refers to the northern and southern extremi-
ies of the Israelite's territory.

The old town of Beersheba was the administrative centre during
he Turkish occupation, and it was here that Lawrence of Arabia
vas imprisoned in World War I after having been convicted of
pying.

HOW TO GET THERE

By Bus
Bus no. 446 from Jerusalem, 393 and 394 from Eilat and 370 from
Tel Aviv.

By Rail
There is a service Tel Aviv-Jerusalem-Beersheba.

By Car
Beersheba is 84km (52 miles) from Jerusalem, 113km (70 miles)
from Tel Aviv and 241km (150 miles) from Eilat.

TOURIST INFORMATION
Israel Government Tourist Office, 120 Herzl Street, ph 057-36
01.

ACCOMMODATION
There's not a lot to choose from, but here are a few names and
addresses, with prices in US Dollars for a double room including
breakfast. The prices should be used as a guide only. The
Telephone Area Code is 057.

Desert Inn, PO Box 247, ph 424 922 — $52–74; Hanegev, 2 Ha'atzmaut Street, ph 77 026 — $30–38; Arava, 37 Ha'histadru Street, ph 78 792 — $28–30; Aviv, 40 Mordei Hagetaot Street, p 78 059 — $26.

LOCAL TRANSPORT
The Central Bus Station is on the north-eastern edge of the Ol Town, near the municipal market.

EATING OUT
Again, there is not much choice, but you might like to try th following:

Bulgarian Restaurant, Karen Kayemet L'Israel — under 20NIS

Chinese Restaurant, 97 Histadrut Street, ph 70 050 — 20–40NIS.

Papa Michel, 95 Histadrut Street, ph 77 298 — Middle Easter — 20–40NIS.

SIGHTSEEING

Negev Museum
Situated at 18 Ha'atzmaut Street, ph 39 105, the museum is in a old Turkish mosque, and is in the centre of the old city. There ar exhibits of the history of the city itself, and other displays o artifacts from the Stone Age, Chalcolithic, Canaanite, Israelite an Byzantine periods. A model of Tel Beersheba, the archeologica site, is also on display.

It is possible to climb to the top of the museum's minaret for panoramic view of the city, but as there is a military installatio across the street, photograhy is not allowed.

In the courtyard there is an excellent collection of Bedoui clothes, tools and artifacts. The museum is open Sun–Thur 8am–2pm, 4.30–7pm, Fri 8am–12.30pm, Sat 10am–1pm.

Abraham's Well
This is one of those places where you have to use your imagine The site is at the southern end of Keren Kayemet Le-Israel Street but the only thing there is a wall. Anyway this is definitel Abraham territory, and if the well isn't actually at this spot, i must be somewhere nearby.

Bedouin Market

The Thursday special show of Beersheba, the market, is held from 6am till noon on the south-eastern edge of town near the municipal marketplace. This is where the Bedouins do their weekly shopping, and where the farmers bring their produce to sell, and they all combine to put on a good show for the tourists. Nevertheless, if you're in town on Thursday don't miss it.

Tel Sheba

The excavations here have unearthed many layers of civilisation. City walls and gates have been revealed, and a circular street with rows of buildings on both sides. Outside the city walls archaeologists have discovered a deep well which was part of the city's canal project. The remains of an ashlar four-horned altar were found here. The altar been reconstructed and is now displayed in the Museum.

At the site there is a visitors' centre with cafeteria, and a small museum. The centre is open daily 9am–11pm, but the tel is always open. Women travelling on their own would be well advised not to accept the offers of locals to guide them around the tel, as they may see more than they bargained for.

Route 40 continues south from Beersheba, and after 30km (19 miles) comes to the Bir Asluj crossroads where a small grove of eucalyptus trees marks the graves of Israeli soldiers killed in 1948 fighting the Egyptians in the battle for the Negev. Nearby are the Kibbutz Mashabbei Sadeh and Moshav Telalim.

Kibbutz Sde Boker

Famous for its peaches and olives, Kibbutz Sde Boker is 13km (8 miles) further south. This kibbutz was founded in 1952, and its most distinguished member was David Ben Gurion, the first prime minister of Israel. He first joined the kibbutz in 1953 after he resigned as prime minister, and as he was sixty-seven at the time there was some resistance because of his inability to do hard physical work. Some years later he returned to office, finally resigned in 1963, and returned to spend the last ten years of his life at Sde Boker. He is buried a few kilometres south of the kibbutz, and the house he lived in has been kept as it was, apart from the addition of a glass wall to keep visitors from his library.

Avdat

Avdat is 10km (6 miles) south of Sde Boker, a 1st century BC Nabatean city. The Nabateans were a desert people who had their capital at Petra (now in Jordan), and built Avdat as a station for their desert caravans carrying spices from Arabia to the Mediterranean ports. They were talented engineers and invented a system of trapping the winter rains and irrigating the land for farming. Botany professor Even-Ari reconstructed a Nabatean farm to prove how their water system worked, and his project can be seen from the top of the hill.

Although many ruins from this period are still to be seen, the most interesting are from the Roman occupation, just after the Nabateans, and from the Byzantine period.

Mitzpe Ramon

22km (14 miles) south of Avdat is the town of Mitzpe Ramon (Ramon Observation Point), which is on the edge of the crater Makhtesh Ramon (Ramon Crater). The crater is 40km (25 miles) long, 9km (5 miles) wide and 400m (1,250 ft) deep. The town was established in 1953, but it is isolated in the middle of the Negev, has no natural resources, and was bypassed by a new road linking Eilat to the Dead Sea. The future of the town was in doubt, then the area was declared a nature reserve and an archeological-geological-ecological park was established, highlighting the unusual rock formations of the crater and offering many hiking trails. There is a Visitors' Centre, open Sun–Thurs 9am–4.30pm, Fri 9am–1.30pm, which is the first part of a big campaign to boost the tourist attractions in the area.

The road crosses the crater, continues south through desert landscapes, to join up with Route 90 about 55km (34 miles) north of Eilat.

EILAT

Israel's southern-most town, Eilat is situated at the tip of the Negev desert on a 5km strip of Red Sea coastline between the Egyptian and Jordanian borders.

The harbour doesn't really measure up to modern standards, but it is one of the great ports in history. Solomon built a fleet of ships here (1 Kings 9:26), and it is thought that this is where the

Queen of Sheba landed when she visited Jerusalem to see Solomon. Eilat flourished as a port from Solomon's time until it was conquered by Saladin in 1167. Its importance dwindled under Muslim rule, although it remained a minor military post until it was taken in a lightning campaign by a small Israeli force in 1949.

The town began to develop after the Suez campaign in 1956. Then the rot set in again. The doubtful future of the Timna copper mines hit the town badly, and the opening of the Suez Canal to Israeli shipping, allowing ships to dock directly at the northern ports of Haifa and Ashdod, almost sounded its death knoll. But with sunshine about 360 days of the year, and the 5km of beaches, tourism was the obvious answer to the problem, and Eilat has become popular as a winter vacation spot for Europeans and Israelis alike.

HOW TO GET THERE

By Air
Arkia, Israel's domestic airline, have several flights daily from Tel Aviv, Jerusalem and Ben Gurion Airport to Eliat.

By Bus
There are bus services from Jerusalem via the Dead Sea; from Tel Aviv, Beersheba and Haifa.

By Car
Eilat is 312km (194 miles) from Jerusalem, 354km (220 miles) from Tel Aviv and 241km (150 miles) from Beersheba.

TOURIST INFORMATION
The Government Tourist Information Office is on Hatmarim Boulevard, opposite the bus station, ph 72 268, and is open Sun–Thurs 8am–6pm, Fri 8am–1pm. There is also a branch in the Neptune Hotel. The office puts out a weekly paper called "Events in Eilat".

ACCOMMODATION
The accommodation charges listed below are in US Dollars for a double room per night with breakfast, and are subject to a 15% service charge. They should be used as a guide only. The Telephone Area Code is 059.

5-star Hotels
King Solomon's Palace, North Beach, ph 79 111 — $129–147; Moriah Eilat, North Beach, ph 72 151 — $118–152; Neptune, North Beach, ph 79 333 — $122–142.

4-star Hotels
New Lagoona, North Beach, ph 79 444 — $129–153; Sport, North Beach, ph 33 333 — $129–153; Shulamit Gardens, North Beach, ph 75 151 — $100; Caesar, North Beach, ph 76 161 — $90; Queen of Sheba, North Beach, ph 72 121 — $85; Red Rock, North Beach, ph 73 141 — $82–98; Galei Eilat, Annex to Neptune, North Shore, ph 73 121 — $80.

3-star Hotels
St Tropez Beach, North Beach, ph 76 111 — $116–139; Coral Sea, Coral Beach, ph 79 555 — $65; Edomit, New Tourist Centre, ph 79 511 — $61; Etzion, Hatmarim Street, ph 74 131 — $60–65; Americana Eilat, P.O. Box 27, North Beach, ph 75 176 — $57.50.

2-star Hotels
Dalia, North Beach, ph 75 127 — $50; Caravan Sun Club, Coral Beach, ph 73 145 — $46–50.

LOCAL TRANSPORT

Bus
Bus 1, 2 and 3 go from the town to the hotel area. Bus 15 runs from the hotel area to the Egyptian border stopping at Coral Beach and Taba. Bus 1A goes from the Eilat Centre opposite the bus station to Sun Bay Camping near the Jordanian border. Bus services are available 6.30am–8pm.

Car
Hiring a car here is an expensive exercise, but if that's the way you like to go, here are a few names and addresses. (Please note — it is not permitted to take a rental car into Egypt.)

Hertz, New Tourist Centre, Yotam Road, ph 76 682.
Inter-Rent, New Tourist Centre, Yotam Road, ph 74 893.
Kopel Rent-A-Car, New Tourist Centre, Yotam Road, ph 74 105.
Avis has their office next to the airport, ph 73 165.
Budget, Etzion Hotel, Hatmarim Boulevard, ph 76 139.
Remember to keep an eye on the radiator because of the extremely hot temperatures.

Bicycle
These can be hired at the Red Sea Sport Centre, ph 71 846, or near the lagoon in front of the Queen of Sheba Hotel.

EATING OUT
As with any other seaside resort, Eilat has plenty to offer in the snack department, with dozens of establishments serving hamburgers and felafels, but there is not much of a choice in the better restaurant range. Here we have listed a few for you to try.

Neve Eilat Restaurant, 103 Hatmarim Boulevard, ph 72 074 — European — open Sun–Thurs, 6am–midnight, Fri 6am–4pm, Sat 6am–sunset — under 20NIS.

Le Bistro, Eilat Street, ph 74 333 — French — over 40NIS.

Ha-Kerem Restaurant, cnr Eilat Street & Hatmarim Boulevard, ph 74 577 — Yemenite — open Sat–Thurs 9am–11pm, Fri 9am–4pm — 20NIS.

Oasis Restaurant, North Beach, ph 72 414 — large menu — open daily noon–midnight — 20NIS.

Last Refuge, Coral Beach, ph 72 437 — seafood — over 40NIS.

ENTERTAINMENT
The Phillip Murray Cultural Center on Hatmarim Boulevard, near the Central Bus Station, has drama and musical (both classic and rock) performances, and the Tourist Information Office will have details of their programmes.

Cinema Eilat, next door to the post office, ph 73 178, is a good place to catch up on a movie that you missed at home.

Most of the major hotels have Israeli Folklore evenings, followed by dancing or a disco, but if you want to give the cultural bit a miss, try the Americana Hotel, ph 75 176, their disco is free.

On the corner of Almogim and Agmonim Streets is the Peace Cafe which is a very popular watering hole.

The Red Lion on level 2 of the New Tourist Centre, has the reputation of being the rowdiest pub in Eilat.

SHOPPING
Forget it.

SIGHTSEEING
The main attraction at Eilat is, of course, the water, and if you are not into scuba diving you should visit the Coral World Under-

water Observatory and Aquarium, ph 73 988, which is a glass-walled complex 100m from shore and 5m below the surface of the water. Here you can get a close-up view of the creatures you're swimming with, such as lionfish, Moray eels and stonefish. Take Bus 15 to its terminus. Open Sat–Thurs 8.30am–5pm, Fri 8.30am–3pm.

Timna Valley National Park

The park is 27km (17 miles) north of Eilat, and has evidence of the area's Bronze Age history. In the south-east corner of the park is the 6,000-year-old Timna Copper Mines from the Egyptian period, with ruins of the workers' camps and cisterns. There are sign-posts from here leading to a wall about 3km away which has ancient carvings of figures in chariots.

Solomon's Pillars, which are huge columns of sandstone, are east of the main road in the park, and nearby are the ruins of a temple dedicated to Hathor, the Egyptian cow goddess.

The Jewish National Fund of America has made the development of the park one of its major projects. United Tours in the Shalom Shopping Centre, ph 74 217, have tours to the park, or take any bus going to Tel Aviv or Jerusalem and ask to be let off at the sign for Alipaz, 2km from the park entrance. The park is open 8am–4pm, and there is a small admission fee.

Hai Bar Wildlife Reserve

40km (25 miles) north of Eilat is the Hai Bar National Biblical Wildlife Reserve, with an area of 3,232ha (8,000 acres). The Reserve was established to save rare and endangered animals mentioned in the Bible, and to repatriate others who are no longer found in Israel. There are gazelles, ostriches and other animals wandering all over the park, but the predators are in large natural enclosures, and include leopards, wolves and striped hyenas. Admission is in a closed vehicle only, so if you don't have a car a tour is the only alternative. The park is open 6am to just before sunset, and feeding time is 8–10.30am. There is an admission fee.

TOURS

Operating out of the North Beach marina, near the Neptune Hotel, are two companies that offer glass-bottom boat tours. Tour Yam Ltd, ph 72 436, have half-day tours to Coral Island, departing from the marina at 9.30am and 2.30pm. They also have hourly boats from the Glass-Bottom Boat Pier on Coral Beach. Israel Yam have daily one-hour tours to Coral Island leaving the marine at 10am, noon and 2pm.

They are several sailboats which offer full-day trips to Coral Island and the Fjord, two points along the Egyptian Sinai coast south of Eilat, but they do not land. Travel agencies and hotel reception desks will make reservations for these tours. One boat is the *Pirate*, ph 72 436, but there are many others.

Although the Sinai is under Egyptian control, it is open to Israeli and foreign tourists coming from Eilat, and there are many tours on offer by the various companies.

Neot Ha-Kihhar Desert Tours have four and five-day treks, and their head office is in Jerusalem at 36 Keren Hayesod Street, ph 02-699 385.

Johnny Desert Tours in the Richter Tourist Centre, Eilat, ph 059-76 777, have several trips on offer.

Arkia Airlines, New Tourist Centre, Eliat, ph 059-76102, have a tour which flies from Eilat, lands near St Catherine's monastery, visits the monastery and Mount Sinai by bus, and flies back to Eilat. This tour is fairly expensive, but remember that it includes about US$20 worth of taxes and fees.

It is possible to get into the Sinai by public bus, but it is only recommended for the very patient, and experienced, traveller. For further information contact the Central Bus Station, Hatmarim Boulevard, ph 059-75 161.

SPORT AND RECREATION
Snorkelling/Scuba Diving
Aqua Sport, opposite the Caravan Sun Club Hotel, Coral Beach, ph 72 788, hire out all equipment, and have diving lessons, diving tours and a divers' hostel. They are open every day.

Raffi Pipson, near the Caravan Sun Club Hotel, Coral Beach, ph 72 909, is an underwater and desert guide, and has all scuba gear for hire.

Venezia, North Beach, ph 73 817 have rowboats, canoes, sailboats, etc, for hire.

Horseriding
Tours on horses from half-day to 4-days can be arranged at Kibbutz Ketura, 40km (25 miles) north of Eilat.

Tennis
Many of the hotels have tennis courts.

GAZA

The Gaza Strip is the land between the Mediterranean and the hills inland, and the Shiqma River to the north and the Besor River to the south. The Strip was held by the Egyptians after 1948, then taken by Israel during the 1956 Suez campaign, then returned to Egypt only to be taken again by the Israelis during the Six Day Way. The area is still under Israeli military rule, and when you take into account the number of Palestinian refugees who live there, and the delicate balance of the political situation, it might be a good idea to think twice about paying a visit.

Gaza was once called Azza, which means 'might' but the Greeks changed it to Gaza, which means 'treasure', because of its strategic position.

The early Egyptians used the town as a base for attacks into Asia, the Hyksons did the same for its attacked into Egypt, and later it became the capital of the Philistine empire.

In 1150 the Crusaders took over and built a large church, which in turn the Mamelukes made into the Great Mosque. So when the modern events took place it really wasn't anything new to this part of the world.

HOW TO GET THERE

By Bus
Take Bus 20 from Ashkelon.

By Car
Gaza is 27km (17 miles) from Ashkelon.

ACCOMMODATION
It is not really recommended that you stay in Gaza, better to make it a day trip from Ashkelon.

SIGHTSEEING

Jammal al-Ikberr (Great Mosque)
Arab tradition says that Samson is buried under this mosque. The Book of Judges (Chapter 16) tells of Samson meeting Delilah in

Gaza, and that was the beginning of the end for him, so who knows? The Arabs also believe that Muhammad's great-grandfather and uncle are also buried here, so maybe they are stretching it a bit. In any case the mosque is open to non-Muslims, except during the five daily prayer sessions.

British War Cemetery
The cemetery is looked after by the British Consulate, and is very well kept. It's very quiet and peaceful here, which is a respite from the rest of the town.

Beaches
The beaches of Gaza are not as crowded as the rest on the Mediterranean Coast, but they are not the cleanest for they catch a lot of tar from the tankers near Ashkelon. Ladies who intend to swim in this area had better invest in a neck-to-knee. And you can forget about moonlight strolls along the beach as there is a dusk-to-dawn curfew.

ASHKELON

Ashkelon was one of the five main cities of the Philistines, the others being Gath, Gaza, Ekron and Ashdod. The Book of Judges (14–16) tells of the hostility between the Israelites and the Philistines, and in the Book of Zephaniah the prophet forecast that Gaza, Ashkelon, Ashdod and Ekron would fall, and that Ashkelon would become a great Israelite city (2:4–7). The local people obviously think that this has happened because the main square in Ashkelon is called Zephaniah Square.

Incidentally, this is where Herod was born.

HOW TO GET THERE

By Bus
Take Bus 300, 301 or 311 from Tel Aviv; Bus 437 from Jerusalem; Bus 363 or 364 from Beersheba.

By Car
Ashkelon is 63km (39 miles) from Tel Aviv; 73km (45 miles) from Jerusalem; 67km (42 miles) from Beersheba.

TOURIST INFORMATION
The Government Tourist Information Office is in Commercial Centre, Afridar, ph (051) 32 412.

ACCOMMODATION
Not a lot to choose from, but the following prices are for a double room, including breakfast in US Dollars, and are subject to a 15% service charge. The Telephone Area Code is 051.

Shulamit Gardens, 11 Hatayassim Street, ph 36 222 — $60; Samson's Gardens, 38 Hatamar Street, Afridar, ph 36 641 — $36.

Club Ashkelon, ph 36 733 offers full board — $125–163.

PUBLIC TRANSPORT
Bus
Bus 13 runs from the Central Bus Station to the beach (July and August).

Bus 3 and 9 run from the Central Bus Station to the park behind the beach.

Bus 4, 5 and 7 pass by Zephania Square in Afridar.

EATING OUT
Most of the popular, inexpensive restaurants are in Migdal, and to get there take Bus 4, 5 or 7 to the station.

You could also try Ma'adan Cafe in the Afridar Centre, ph 31 925 — lunch and dinner — 20NIS, or Restaurant Mario, 101 Hatayasim Street, Barnea — lunch and dinner — 25NIS.

The Central Bus Station has a cafeteria which has very reasonably priced food.

ENTERTAINMENT
The most popular watering hole for young Israelis is The Village House in Afridar Square, near the clock tower.

Every night on Delilah Beach there is a barbecue, enjoyed by locals and visitors alike.

Films in English are shown at the Rachel Cinema in Zephania Square, ph 31 429, and the Esther Cinema in the Givat Zion district, ph 22 659.

New Synagogue, Capernaum

Jericho

Dead Sea

Haifa.

SIGHTSEEING

Beaches

There are several public beaches, but all tend to have irregular currents, and it is best to swim only when there is a lifeguard on duty.

The National Park's beach is at the southernmost edge of the city and has grass lawns and impressive Roman ruins of pillars, columns and statues.

Delilah Beach has three small islands within wading distance. North Beach offers nude bathing, but no lifeguards.

Unfortunately, these beaches are also affected by the tar substance from the tankers, so if you end up with black feet, try turps or cooking oil.

Roman Tombs

There are pieces of the wall of the 12th century Crusader city along the southern edge of the National Park, and remains of the Roman columns used to strengthen an ancient Byzantine sea wall.

At the northern end of the beach is a Roman tomb, believed to have been built for a wealthy Hellenistic family in the 3rd century. Inside there are very well-preserved frescoes. The tomb is open Sun–Fri 9am–1pm, Sat 10am–2pm.

Kibbutz Yad Mordechai

The kibbutz, which was established in 1943, is south of Ashkelon on Route 4. It is named after Mordechai Anilewicz, leader of the Warsaw Ghetto uprising against the Nazis in World War II, and was the scene of resistance itself during the 1948 War of Independence. There is a reconstruction of this battle in the kibbutz, with explanations in several languages.

Nearby is a museum dedicated to Jewish Resistance in Poland. The museum is open Sun–Thurs 8am–4pm, Fri 8am–2pm, closed Saturday, and there is a small admission fee. Take Bus 19 from Ashkelon.

Qiryat Gat

About 22km (14 miles) east of Ashkelon, Qiryat Gat is named after the Biblical town of Gat, the birthplace of Goliath, which is thought to have been on the nearby hill. There have been many excavations carried out in the area, but there is nothing much of interest to see.

Tel Lakhish

On the way from Qiryat Gat to Bet Guvrin there are ruins of a Crusader castle, and at about the half way mark there is a walking track leading to Tel Lakhish, an ancient city which the Bible tells Joshua took in battle (Joshua 10:31–32). Probably because of its stragic position, Lakhish has been the site of many periods of settlement, and excavations have established nine different occupancies, but unfortunately most items of interest have been taken to various museums, not leaving much on show at the site itself.

Bet Guvrin

Further east on Route 35 is Kibbutz Bet Guvrin, which is surrounded by about 4000 caves, some of which are natural limestone, but others were probably made by the Phoenicians when they dug the limestone for construction of the port of Ashkelon between the 4th and 7th centuries. Later the caves were used by hermits and monks, and it is thought that St John spent some time here.

A side road to the right off Route 35 at Bet Guvrin leads to Tel Maresha, where there are more caves, some of which have rather elaborate staircases leading to well below ground level. To the east of the Tel are two Sidonian burial tombs dating back to the 2nd century BC.

ASHDOD

Ashdod was another of the five great Philistine cities. It was also inhabited by the Greeks, who called it Azotus, and the Maccabees, and then Arabs, who called it Isdud. Ashdod was the site of a decisive battle during the 1948 War of Independence.

The modern town was virtually dredged out of the sand in 1957, and the deep water port has absorbed much of the shipping from Haifa and caused the closure of Tel Aviv's port.

HOW TO GET THERE

By Bus

Ashdod is connected by bus to Tel Aviv, Ashkelon, Beersheba and Jerusalem.

By Car

Ashdod is 33km (20 miles) from Ashkelon, 42km (26 miles) from Tel Aviv, and 66km (41 miles) from Jerusalem.

ACCOMMODATION

There are two hotels in Ashdod, so not really much choice here. They are:

Miami, 12 Nordau Street, ph (08) 522 0856.

Orly, Nordau Street, ph (08) 531 549.

Both hotels offer a double room, breakfast included, for US$50 per night.

EATING OUT

The usual felafel stands, or else the hotels.

SIGHTSEEING

As you may have gathered, Ashdod is not really a tourist town, but if you find yourself in the vicinity there are a couple of interesting things to see.

Yaffa Ben-Ami Memorial Hill

The Muslims believe that the ruins on this hill are of Jonah's tomb, but whether or not, there is a fine view of the town and its surroundings.

Fatamid Fortress

On the southern edge of the city are the remains of a pre-Crusader fortress. Documents have been found by archaeologists which show that Ashdod was a port in Byzantine times. It is still possible to see the four towers, but the rest of the site is nothing to get excited about.

Market

Every Wednesday there is a full day market on Lido Beach.

Rishon Le-Ziyyon

On Route 4 north from Ashdod travelling towards Tel Aviv is Rishon Le-Ziyyon, one of the main centres of the Israel wine industry. There are guided tours of the vineyards, which were started by Russian immigrants in 1882, and came to the attention of Baron de Rothschild of France, who provided the much-needed finance for their success.

TEL AVIV

The largest city in Israel, and its business, financial, cultural an entertainment centre, Tel Aviv is a bustling metropolis, and hom to a quarter of the country's population.

It has very good beaches and its share of museums, parks an markets. Generally speaking, it is an unattractive city, and it lifestyle is completely the opposite to Jerusalem. If the visitor h. had enough of 'holy', Tel Aviv is the place to go.

The establishment of Tel Aviv began in 1909 when people le the crowded old city of Jaffa to begin a new city to the north. Th new city grew beyond their wildest dreams, until it joined with tl old, and in 1950 Tel Aviv and Jaffa were combined into one city

HISTORY

Jaffa lays claim to being the oldest port in the world, having bein founded by Japhet, the son of Noah. Egyptian records have bee unearthed which show that Jaffa was conquered by Pharoa Thutmoses III when he went to put down a revolt in the Jezre' Valley. Archaeologists working in old Jaffa have also discovere inscriptions with the name of Pharoah Ramses II.

It was to Jaffa (Joppa) that Hiram, king of Tyre, brought tl cedars from Lebanon for the building of Solomon's Temp (2 Chron.2:16), and it was from Joppa that Jonah started h voyage and adventure with the whale (Jonah 1:3). St Peter w; called to Jaffa when Tabitha died, and he raised her from the dea (Acts 9:36–43).

Greek legend claims that it was to one of the rocks near the o port that Poseidon, the god of the seas, chained Andromeda, wh was rescued by Perseus.

Jaffa became a great port under Solomon's rule, and was lat controlled by the Phoenicians and then the Greeks. It was tl Greeks who killed the Jewish community during the Maccabe; revolt in 165BC, and in retaliation the Maccabees burned the city

During the reign of Herod the Great, Jaffa faded into oblivic and Caesarea became the major port. Then in the 12th centur

uring the Crusades, it regained its importance. It was alternately
won and lost by the Crusaders, and finally came under Arab
ontrol when the Mamelukes took the city in 1267. They managed
o hold it, except for a brief period when Napoleon was on the
narch, until defeated by British General Allenby in 1917.

Meanwhile the 19th century saw an influx of European Jewish
nmigrants, which did not entirely please the local Arab popula-
on. Some of the Jews decided to start a settlement to the north,
which they first called Ahuzat Bayit and later became Tel Aviv,
ut this did not please the Arabs either, so there was continual
nti-Jewish rioting and general unrest. During the early part of
World War I the Turks deported many of the residents of Tel
Aviv, and the entire town was evacuated. But Arab riots in Jaffa in
921 and 1929 caused more and more Jews to abandon Jaffa for the
elative safety of Tel Aviv.

HOW TO GET THERE

By Air

nternational passengers arrive at Ben Gurion Airport near Tel
Aviv, and details of flights is given in the "Travel Information"
hapter.

United Tours, ph 432 414, run buses from the airport to the air
erminal on Harakevet Street from 5am–midnight.

Taxis and sheruts are also easily hired from the airport.

By Bus

There are frequent bus services to Tel Aviv from Jerusalem, Haifa
nd Beersheba. The central bus station is large and confusing, so
n arrival it is a good idea to find out where the bus leaves from for
our next destination. You may be short of time when leaving, and
t can be very frustrating if you can't find the right bus.

By Car

Tel Aviv is 62km (39 miles) from Jerusalem, 117km (73 miles)
rom Acre, 63km (39 miles) from Ashkelon, 219km (136 miles)
rom Eilat and 95km (59 miles) from Haifa.

By Train

Tel Aviv has two railway stations. The service from Jerusalem-
Haifa arrives at the South railway station on Kibbutz Galuyot
Boulevard.

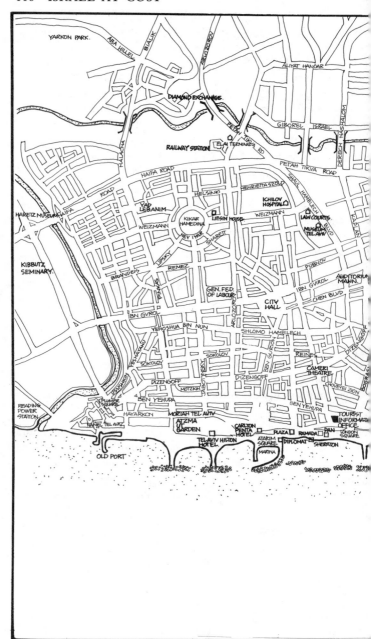

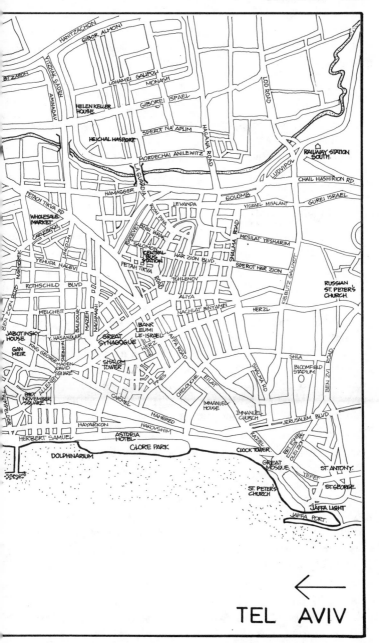

TEL AVIV

The Central railway station is at the junction of Haifa Road, Arlosoroff Street and Petah Tiqwa Road, and is used by trains coming from Haifa and the northern towns.

TOURIST INFORMATION
The Israel Government Tourist Office is at 7 Mendele Street, ph 223 266, and is open Sun–Thurs 8.30am–5pm, Fri 8.30am–2pm, closed Saturday.

The Tourist Office will also have copies of "Events in the Tel Aviv Region" and "This Week in Israel", free leaflets with all the current happenings.

ACCOMMODATION
There are so many hotels to choose from that price may make the final decision. Here we have listed a selection, with prices in US Dollars for a double room, including breakfast, per night and subject to a 15% service charge. The Telephone Area Code is 03.

5-star Hotels
Tel Aviv Sheraton, 115 Hayarkon Street, ph 286 222 — $125–180; Tel Aviv Hilton, Independence Park ph 546 444 — $154; Dan Tel Aviv, 99 Hayarkon Street, ph 241 111 — $126–148; Moriah Plaza, 155 Hayarkon Street, ph 299 555 — $110–122; Ramada Continental, 121 Hayarkon Street, ph 296 444 — $110; Carlton Tel Aviv, 10 Morad Hayarkon, ph 291 291 — $106–126; Dan Panorama, 10 Y. Kaufman Street, ph 663 311 — $92–102.

4-star Hotels
Grand Beach, 250 Hayarkon Street, ph 436 6555 — $93; Avia, B.G. International Airport Area, ph 352 221 — $74; Basel, 156 Hayarkon Street, ph 244 161 — $73; Tal, 287 Hayarkon Street, ph 455 281 — $68; Astor, 105 Hayarkon Street, ph 223 141 — $64–69; Kfar Maccabiah, Ramat Gan, ph 715 715 — $65; Ramat Aviv, 151 Derech Namir, ph 413 181 — $63–69; Sinai, 11–15 Trumpeldor Street, ph 652 621 — $60–70; Park, 75 Hayarkon Street, ph 651 551 — $55.

3-star Hotels
City, 9 Mapu Street, ph 246 253 — $64; Adiv, 5 Mendele Street, ph 229 141 — $55; Ambassador, 2 Allenby Street, ph 510 3993 —$53; Florida, 164 Hayarkon Street, ph 242 184 — $50; Ami,

4 Am Israel Hai Street, ph 249 141 — $50; Shalom, 216 Hayarkon Street, ph 243 277 — $50; Ora, 35 Ben Yehuda Street, ph 650 941 — $40–44; Maxim, 86 Hayarkon Street, ph 653 721 — $38–40.

2-star Hotels
Armon Hayarkon, 268 Hayarkon Street, ph 455 271 — $45; Moss, 6 Ness Ziona Street, ph 651 655 — $45; Imperial, 66 Hayarkon Street, ph 657 002 — $39.

LOCAL TRANSPORT

Bus
Public buses run frequently to all the major tourist attractions (except on the Sabbath) and there are set fares.

United Tours run a special service linking Hayarkon Street on the beach to the Herzilya hotel area.

Taxi
Sherut services run from Salomon Street, opposite the central bus station, to the suburbs, Jerusalem and Haifa, Sun–Fri. On Saturday they run from Moshavot Square.

Car
The following rental companies have offices in Tel Aviv: Avis, 75 Hayarkon Street, ph 651 093; Budget, 74 Derech Petach Tikva, ph 336 126; Gan-Car, 100 Hayarkon Street, ph 225 772; Hertz, 81 Hayarkon Street, ph 656 248; Thrifty, 126 Atarim Square, ph 283 281.

EATING OUT

Tel Aviv is the restaurant capital of Israel, and whatever your taste, you certainly won't go hungry. Here we list a some you might like to try, with prices for a main meal as a guide.

Alhambra, 30 Jerusalem Boulevard, Jaffa, ph 834 453 — French — over 40NIS.

Beriozka, 77 Ben Yehuda Street, ph 223 355 — Russian — over 40NIS.

Bucaresti, 52 Chen Boulevard, ph 262 922 — Romanian — over 40NIS.

Keren, 13 Ibn Bvirol Street, ph 224 553 — Continental — over 40NIS.

Pink Ladle, 15 Balfour Street, ph 202 302 — French — over 40NIS.

Shaldag, 256 Ben Yehuda Street, ph 445 465 — Seafood — over 40NIS.

Toutoun, 1 Mazal Dagim Street, ph 820 693 — French — over 40NIS.

L'Entrecot, 193 Ben Yehuda Street, ph 230 726 — Steak — 20–40NIS.

Fisherman's, 12 Jaffa Port, ph 813 870 — Seafood — 20–40NIS.

Front Page, 252 Ben Yehuda Street, ph 455 377 — Italian — 20–40NIS.

Gan Shickman, 8 Nachamia Street, ph 663 066 — Israeli — 20–40NIS.

Mandy's Singing Bamboo, 317 Hayarkon Street, ph 451 282 — 20–40NIS.

Pizzafina, 169 Ben Yehuda Street, ph 239 582 — Italian — 20–40NIS.

Red Chinese Restaurant, 326 Dizengoff Street, ph 448 408 — 20–40NIS.

Stern Dolphin, 189 Dizengoff Street, ph 232 425 — Seafood — 20–40NIS.

Taj Mahal, Kikar Hedumim, Old Jaffa, ph 821 002 — Indian — 20–40NIS.

Yin Yang, 64 Rothschild Boulevard, ph 621 833 — Chinese — 20–40NIS.

French Crepe, 134 Dizengoff Street, ph 233 436 — under 20NIS.

Goulash Corner, 108 Hayarkon Street, ph 236 859 — Hungarian — under 20NIS.

Me and Me, 49 Bograshov Street, ph 287 382 — Middle-Eastern — under 20NIS.

Misu, 7 Raziel Street — Romanian — under 20NIS.

The Stage Coach, 216 Hayarkon Street, ph 241 703 — Hamburgers — under 20NIS.

There are also literally hundreds of coffee shops and snackbars, and nearly all serve light meals. Eating at these can be a good way of meeting the locals, who are very friendly to visitors — just don't talk politics.

Mention was made before that Tel Aviv is not as 'holy' as Jerusalem, and consequently many of the cafes and bars are open on Friday nights, and in fact are usually very busy. And if you still want that cheeseburger you couldn't get in Jerusalem, the local MacDavid's (at 39 Frishman Street) will oblige.

ENTERTAINMENT

Tel Aviv has plenty to offer for night-time entertainment. Every Friday the newspaper *The Jerusalem Post* has a *Metro* supplement giving details of what's on and where in Tel Aviv.

The top hotels have bars, discos and night clubs, and 'Little Tel Aviv', near the intersections of Ben Yehuda and Dizengoff Streets with Yirmiyahu and Yordei Hasira Streets in the northern part of the city, is crammed with restaurants and bars. Old Jaffa is also extremely busy at night with dozens of night clubs with floorshows.

Here are a few to select from:

Michel's Aladdin, 5 Mifraz Shlomo Street, ph 826 766.

Le Club, cnr Ben Yehuda and Yirmiyahu Streets.

Harimta Theatre/Cafe, 8 Mazal Dagim Street.

Omar Khayam, Kedumim Square, Old Jaffa.

The Penguin Club, 43 Yehuda Halevi Street.

The Mann Auditorium on Habima Square, ph 295 092, is the headquarters of the Israel Philharmonic Orchestra, and the information desk at your hotel may be able to arrange tickets for one of their often-sold-out performances.

The Cameri Theatre, 101 Dizengoff Street, ph 222 995, and the Habima Theatre, Habima Square, ph 283 742, present plays in Hebrew, but visitors can rent headphones for translations by professional actors.

The Jerusalem Post has details of all cinema programmes. Movies are often in English with Hebrew sub-titles.

SHOPPING

Tel Aviv has two large department stores — Shalom in the Shalom Tower and Hamashbir in Dizengoff Centre. The prices may be a bit steeper in these stores than in the markets, but the quality is guaranteed.

The Shalom Tower also has numerous boutiques, and their wares are made on the premises.

In the vicinity of Magen David Square there are two street markets. The Carmel Market is, naturally enough, on Carmel Street, and is the most colourful and crowded. The other is the Bezalel Market, between King George and Tchernichovsky Streets. Both are good places to pick up souvenirs and cheap clothing.

Strange as it may seem, Tel Aviv is a good place to buy fur products, and because of the tax concessions for tourists, the prices are very competitive. The main area for furriers is along Allenby Road and Ben Yehuda Street.

Most of the city's galleries are on Gordon Street, or in Old Jaffa, and they don't only stock religious art.

The Jaffa Fleamarket is worth a visit, and who knows, amongst all the junk there may be a priceless antique.

SIGHTSEEING

There's quite a lot to see in Tel Aviv-Jaffa, so let's begin at Old Jaffa, the most interesting, and work our way north to the Yarkon River.

Old Jaffa

The best place to start is the Ottoman Clock Tower, at the intersection of Jerusalem and Mifratz Shlomo Streets. In fact there are free walking tours starting from here every Wednesday at 9.30am run by the Association for Tourism of Tel Aviv-Yafo. To the right and up the hill is Old Jaffa, to the left is the flea market, and straight ahead is Yefet Street, which has mainly Arab bakeries and sweet shops.

On top of the hill is Kikar Kedumim, the central plaza, dominated by the Franciscan Monastery of St Peter, built above a medieval citadel. The monastery is open on Sunday for prayers. Kikar Kedumim was the site of the city's first Jewish hostel, which included two mikvehs (ritual baths) and a synagogue, which has been re-opened.

At the foot of the steps on the southern side of Kikar Kedumim, is the house of Simon the Tanner (8 Shimon Ha-Burski Street, ph 836 792). This is where St Peter was staying when he received instructions to preach to non-Jews (Acts 9:43–10:23). The house is open daily 8am–6.30pm, and there is a small admission fee.

The Museum of Antiquities of Tel Aviv-Jaffa is at 10 Mifratz Shlomo Street, ph 825 373, and the building was a Turkish administrative and detention centre during the 19th century (note the beautifully preserved vaulted ceilings and archways). The exhibits are from local excavations, and range from 5000BC to the Arab period (about 1000AD). The museum is open Sun–Fri 9am–1pm, Tues 4–7pm, Sat 10am–1pm, and there is an admission fee.

Behind the museum are the HaPisga Gardens with a small amphitheatre, and an archaeological site, with parts of a wall built in the 13th century BC by the Hyksos rulers of Egypt, and the remains of the city gate bearing the name of Ramses II. Excavations have also uncovered a Canaanite city, a Jewish city from the time of Ezra, a 3rd century BC wall, a statue of Aphrodite, and Hasmonean and Roman ruins. On one hill there is a white sculpture in the neo-Mayan style, depicting the fall of Jericho, Isaac's near-sacrifice and Jacob's dream.

From the lighthouse there is a good view of Andromeda's Rock, the most prominent of the blackened stones jutting out of the water in the harbour.

Neve Tzedek

A Jewish neighbourhood, just north of Jaffa, Neve Tzedek predates Tel Aviv and was founded by Shimon Rokach. His house has been restored and is now a gallery and coffee shop. The whole area is gaining the reputation of being an artists' colony, and in the small streets, to the north, there are workshops of clothing designers, where it is possible to pick up a bargain.

Shalom Tower

The 125m (410 ft) tower was built in 1959 on the site of the Gymnasia Herzlia, the first secular, Hebrew-language secondary school in Israel. The tower includes a post office branch, supermarket, department store, the Ministry of the Interior's offices, an observatory and a wax museum. There is a panoramic view from the observatory, but there's not much to see, and the wax museum certainly isn't anything to rave about. Anyway, the museum and observatory are open Sept–May Sun–Thurs 9am–4.30pm, Fri 9am–1.30pm, June–Aug Sun–Fri 9am–6.45pm, and there is an admission fee.

Great Synagogue

On the corner of Allenby Road and Ahad Ha'am Street, the synagogue was built in 1926 and renovated in 1970. It is most impressive on Friday at sunset when the crowds of people making their way to the temple bring the traffic to a standstill.

Ben Gurion's House

Ben Gurion, Israel's first prime minister, lived in this house-cum-museum at 17 Ben Gurion Avenue, and exhibits here include letters and tributes from all over the world. Open Sun–Fri 8am–1pm, Mon and Thurs 5–7pm, Sat 11am–2pm and there is no admission fee.

Jabotinsky Institute

On the first floor of the Institute, 38 King George Street, ph 287 320, is a museum presenting the history and achievements of the National Resistance Movement, which was founded by Za'ev Jabotinsky. There are also exhibits from the creation of the Jewish Legion in World War I, and the Revisionist Movement with their illegal immigration programme. The museum is open Sun, Tues, Thurs 10am–6pm, Mon and Wed 10am–1pm and 6–8pm, Fri 10am–1pm, and there is no admission fee.

Beit Bialik Museum

Hayim Naman Bialik was one of Israel's greatest poets, and the museum is in the house where he died, which has been left untouched. All his work, including paintings, photographs, articles, letters and books (which have been translated in 28 languages) are on display. The museum is in Bialik Street, off Allenby Road, and is open Sun–Thurs 9am–7pm, Fri 9am–1pm and there is no entrance fee.

Hagana Museum

The former home of Eliyahu Golomb, once a Hagana general, the museum is at 23 Rothschild Boulevard, ph 623 624. The exhibits record the history of the Israeli Defence Force from the beginning of the century to the War of Independence. The museum is open Sun–Fri 9am–3pm, and there is an admission fee.

Independence Hall

It was in this hall, at 16 Rothschild Boulevard, on May 14, 1948, that Ben Gurion declared the establishment of the State of Israel. The hall was then part of the old Tel Aviv Museum, but it had previously been the home of Meir Dizengoff, the first mayor of Tel Aviv. Open Sun–Fri 9am–1pm, ph 653 942, and there is an admission fee.

Founders' Monument

In the centre of the island at Nahlat Benyamin Street and Rothschild Boulevard is the Founders' Monument, which depicts the three phases of Tel Aviv's history — the first field workers of 1909; the Herzlia Gymnasium; modern Tel Aviv with the Habima Theatre, Bialik House and modern apartment buildings.

Habima Square

The cultural centre of Tel Aviv, the square links Rothschild Boulevard with Dizengoff Street and Ibn Gevirol. Here are found the Habima Theatre and the Mann Auditorium, and around the corner at 6 Tarsat Boulevard is the Helena Rubinstein Pavilion, which has changing exhibits by Israeli and overseas artists. The pavilion is open Mon–Thurs 10am–1pm and 5–7pm, Sat 11am–2pm, ph 287 196. Sometimes, depending on the exhibition, there is an admission fee, but a Tel Aviv Museum ticket will cover it.

Tel Aviv Museum

Located at 27 King Saul Boulevard is the Tel Aviv Museum which has a large collection of international and Israeli art. The museum is very large, so if you are into art allow yourself plenty of time. If you want a quick trip, try Pavilion 2 which has a collection of Impressionist art, including works by Renior, Corot, Monet, Duffy and Pissaro, and Post-Impressionists such as Picasso, Kokoschka, Roualt and Matisse. The *Jerusalem Post* has details of current special exhibitions. Open Sun–Thurs 10am–2pm and 5–9pm, Sat 11am–2pm. The admission fee also covers the Helena Rubinstein Pavilion.

The Diaspora Museum

Beit Hatfusot, the Diaspora Museum, is on the campus of Tel Aviv University, in Ramat Aviv, north of the Yarkon River. It is without doubt the most popular museum in Tel Aviv, with its unique modern techniques, including dioramas, audio-visual displays and computers. Its theme is Jewish communities and family life in exile. Open Sun–Tues and Thurs 10am–5pm, Wed

10am–7pm. There is an admission fee. Take Bus 25 from Jaffa, Carmel Market or the youth hostel, or Bus 27 from the Central Bus Station.

Beaches

The long stretch of white sand beach is one of Tel Aviv's main attractions, and is within walking distance of Dizengoff Square, and most of the accommodation, shops and restaurants. As the weather is very accommodating, the beaches are usually very crowded, particularly in the area between the Hilton and the beginning of Allenby Road, and theft is a problem, so don't take any valuables with you when you go for a swim.

Also, Tel Aviv beaches have a high tally of drownings, due to an unpredictable undertow, so unless you are a particularly strong swimmer, it is best to stick to the patrolled areas. Here it is not just a case of swimming between the flags — there is a system of different coloured flags denoting the water conditions. Black means the area is closed to swimming, Red means use caution, and White indicates everything's OK.

Another word of warning for the ladies — this is not the place to wear your brief bikini. If you do, it won't only be skin cancer you will have to worry about, there'll also be the annoying attention of the local men. In fact, if you want to swim and sunbake in perfect peace, try the religious beach north of the Hilton on Sun, Tues and Thurs, when only women are allowed in that area.

Probably the cleanest beach is at Clore Park to the south, where there are barbecue facilities.

Most of the beaches have free showers and change rooms.

Safari Park

In the suburb of Ramat Gan, the 100ha (250 acre) Safari Park is of the open-range variety. Buses 30, 35 and 45 from anywhere in Tel Aviv go to the park, but entry is allowed only in closed vehicles. With this type of park, I think it is a case of see one and you've seen them all. Anyway, it is open daily 9am–4pm (6pm in summer and 2pm Fri).

SPORT AND RECREATION

Swimming
Most of the hotels have pools, and there is a large public pool at Gordon Street. The best area for windsurfing is opposite the Astoria Hotel, and equipment is available there for hire.

Tennis
Several courts are found on Rokach Boulevard, including the Maccabi, Hapoel and Israel Tennis Centre. Your hotel will be able to book a court for you.

Squash
Herzlia Squash Club, Shivat Hakochavim Boulevard, Herzlia, ph 052-557877, has eight courts available for hire.

Boating
Sailing boats are available for hire at the Tel Aviv Marina, near Atarim Square. You can hire boats for rowing on the Yarkon River at the northern end of Ibn Gvirol Street.

TOURS
There are three main tour companies in Tel Aviv — Egged Tours, 15 Frishman Street, ph 244 177; Galilee Tours, 142 Hayarkon Street, ph 225 817; United Tours, 113 Hayarkon Street, ph 754 333. Tours leave Tel Aviv daily to all parts of the country. Most of the tours listed in the Jerusalem Tours section also leave from Tel Aviv for a slightly higher price, but here are a couple of Galilee Tours which originate exclusively in Tel Aviv.

Tour 226 — 2 days — departing 8am Wed, Thurs.
First stop Jerusalem for a 3 hour tour of the Old City, then visit the Mt of Olives, the Model of Jerusalem, Yad Vashem, the Knesset, the Garden of Gethsemane, the Church of All Nations, Mary's Tomb, the Garden Tomb and Rachel's Tomb. Then on to Bethlehem and the Church of the Nativity — 4-star hotel, half board — US$120.

Tour 237 — 2 days — departing 8am daily, except Wed and Thurs.
First day — Jerusalem Old City, Bethlehem, overnight in Jerusalem.
Second day — Masada, Dead Sea and Jericho OR Masada, Dead Sea and Ein Gedi — 4-star hotel, half board — US$125.

OUTLYING ATTRACTIONS

BAT YAM
A popular beach resort, Bat Yam means 'Daughter of the Sea' and is on the southern fringes of Tel Aviv-Jaffa.

HOW TO GET THERE
By Bus
Take Bus 10, 18, 25 or 26 from Tel Aviv, and the trip can take from 5 minutes to 20, depending what part of Tel Aviv you start from.

By Car
Jerusalem Boulevard leads south from Tel Aviv, through Jaffa, and becomes Rothschild Boulevard, Bat Yam's main street.

TOURIST INFORMATION
The Municipal Tourist Information Bureau, ph 589 766, is a few doors north of the Ben Gurion-Rothschild Boulevards intersection, in the same building as the Via Maris Hotel and the Kontiki Restaurant. Open Sun–Thurs 8am–6.30pm.

ACCOMMODATION
Most of the hotels in Bat Yam are on Ben Gurion Boulevard, facing the sea, and as that is the main attraction here, what better place? Here we have listed just a few, with prices for a double room per night, with breakfast, in US Dollars. The Telephone Area Code is 03.

Armon Yam (4-star), 95 Ben Gurion Boulevard, ph 552 2424 —$45; Via Maris (3-star), 43 Ben Gurion Boulevard, ph 860 171 — $37; Sarita (1-star), 127 Ben Gurion Boulevard, ph 552 9183 — $30.

HERZLIA
Herzlia was named in memory of Theodor Herzl and is one of the most famous beach resorts in Israel. It was founded in 1924 as an agricultural centre, but with the growth of Tel Aviv, the beaches became more accessible, and Herzlia is now a part of the lifestyle of the rich and famous.

HOW TO GET THERE

By Bus

Egged have a service Tel Aviv-Herzlia. United Tours Bus 90 leaves from the Panorama Hotel in Tel Aviv, takes under 40 minutes to reach Herzlia, and runs on the Sabbath. From the town of Herzlia, bus 29 or 90 run to the beach area.

By Car

Herzlia is 16km (10 miles) north of Tel Aviv.

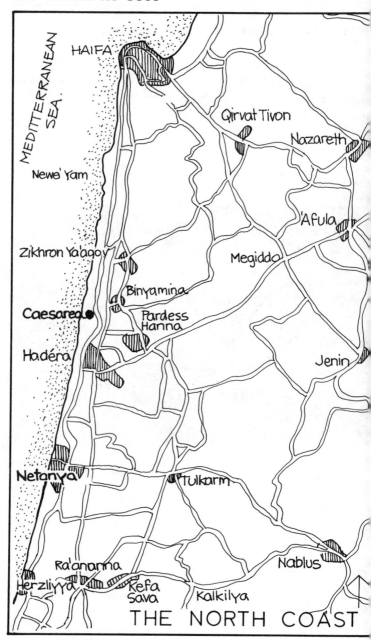

THE NORTH COAST

THE NORTH COAST

NETANYA

Netanya is a popular seaside resort and the capital of the Sharon Plain, the rich citrus-growing area which stretches from the outskirts of Tel Aviv to Caesarea in the north. The town was founded in 1929, and was named after Nathan Straus, a philanthropist who owned Macy's department store in North York at the turn of the century.

The Sharon district is also an industrial centre with diamond-cutting the most important undertaking. After World War II, Jewish diamond-cutters brought the art to Israel, and now it is the world's largest exporter of cut and polished diamonds, with Netanya one of the major centres.

Netanya is also home to the country's only brewery.

HOW TO GET THERE

By Bus

Buses 601 and 605 leave from Tel Aviv for Netanya about every fifteen minutes until 11.30pm. There are also services from Jerusalem and Ben Gurion Airport every 30 minutes.

There are also services from Beersheba and Eilat.

By Car

Netanya is 34km (21 miles) north of Tel Aviv along the Haifa Road.

By Train

The Haifa-Tel Aviv and Haifa-Jerusalem services stop at Netanya.

TOURIST INFORMATION

The Government Tourist Information Office is on the south-western corner of Ha-Atzma'ut Square, ph 27 286, and is open Sun–Thurs 8.30am–2pm and 4–7pm, Fri 8.30am–2pm.

The Municipal Tourist Office is at Kikar Tzion, 2 blocks west on Herzl Street, open Sun–Thurs 9am–1pm and 5–7pm, Fri 9am–1pm.

There is a monthly booklet "Kan Netanya" which lists enter
tainment, special events and services in Netanya.

ACCOMMODATION

Mention has been made of the fact that Netanya is a popula
seaside resort, so as would be expected, there is a wide range o
accommodation. As usual the prices here are for a double room
with breakfast, in US Dollars, and should be used as a guide only
The Telephone Area Code is 053.

5-star Hotel

The Seasons, Nice Boulevard, ph 618 555 — $150.

4-star Hotels

Blue Bay, 37 Hamelachim Street, ph 623 322 — $80; Gaul, 26 Nic
Boulevard, ph 624 455 — $70; Park, 7 David Hamelech Street, ph
623 344 — $64; King Solomon, 18 Hamaapilim Street, ph 338 444
— $63; Goldar, 1 Usishkin Street, ph 336 188 — $54; Beit Ami, 41
Shlomo Hamelech, ph 611 222 — $54; Metropol Grand, 17 Gad
Makhnes Street, ph 624 777 — $53.

3-star Hotels

Residence, 18 Gad Makhnes Street, ph 623 777 — $56; Princess, 28
Gad Makhnes Street, ph 622 666 — $52; Sironit, 19 Gad Machnes
Street, ph 340 688 — $50; Topaz, 25 King David Street, ph 624 555
— $50; Orly, 20 Hamaapilim Street, ph 333 091 — $50; King
David Palace, 4 King David Street, ph 342 151 — $50; Maxim, 8
King David Street, ph 339 341 — $46; Hof, 9 Ha'atzmaut Square,
ph 624 422 — $46; Palace, 33 Gad Makhnes Street, ph 620 222 —
$44; Galei Hasharon, 42 Ussishkin Street, ph 341 946 — $34.

2-star Hotels

Gali-Zans, 6 Ha'melachim Street, ph 621 777 — $57; Ginot-Yam,
9 David Hamelech Street, ph 341 007 — $38; Margoa-B, 4–9 Gad
Makhnes Street, ph 624 434 — $37; Atzmauth, 2 Ussishkin Street,
ph 22 562 — $33; The House, 25 Ussishkin Street, ph 23 107 —
$31; Mitzpe-Yam, 4 Karlibach Street, ph 623 730 — $28; Gal Yam,
46 Dizengoff Street, ph 22 603 — $26.

LOCAL TRANSPORT

It is possible to get everywhere you would want to go by foot,
however if you are arriving by train, you will need to get a bus to
the Central Bus Station downtown.

EATING OUT

There are many sidewalk cafes in Ha-Atzma'ut Square and along Herzl Street, and as in any country in the world, the most crowded will probably be the best. Here are a few you might like to try.

Pundak Ha Yam Grill Bar, 1 HaRav Kook Street, ph 24 880 — grills and salads — open noon–midnight (Fri noon–3.30pm) — 10NIS.

Renaissance Restaurant, 6 Ha-Atzma'ut Square, ph 28 653 — Israeli — open daily 11am–11pm — 10–20NIS.

Restaurant Miamij, 2 Herzl Street, ph 32 600 — Middle Eastern — open Sun–Thurs 9am–midnight, Fri 9am–4.30pm, Sat 6pm–midnight — 10NIS.

Mini Golf Restaurant and Pub, 21 Nice Boulevard, ph 23 109 —grills & Italian — open till 4am — 10NIS.

ENTERTAINMENT

Netanya has a lot to offer at night, but most of it geared to the older visitor. For example, there is Bingo at the American and Canadian Association, 28 Schmuel Ha-Naziv Street, ph 30 950, every Sunday at 8pm, and Duplicate Bridge every Monday and Thursday at 8.15pm at the Women's League House, 5 MacDonald Street. At the Library, 30 Shmuel Ha-Naziv Street, the Chess Club hold its meetings every Monday 7–10pm.

But, if the above is not your scene, you can try The Place, next door to the Whitman Restaurant. It's really two Places — a nightclub and a piano bar. The nightclub is the modern disco type, but the piano bar can be a bit dodgy, with for example, Israeli folk singing, but it's a case of whatever turns you on. Admission to both is for the one price of about 15NIS, but at last the ladies win because they get in free.

A popular pub at 14 Herzl Street is The Magnet, which serves snacks and has a piano bar.

There is community folk dancing every Saturday, April to end of October, in Ha-Atzma'ut Square starting at 8am. They get quite a large crowd and it's free.

SHOPPING

Of course, the obvious things to shop for are diamonds, and they are certainly cheaper than back home. Even if your budget doesn't stretch to these beautiful stones, it is very interesting to visit one of the diamond centres all of which have free tours and exhibitions.

The Netanya Diamond Centre has two locations — 31 Benjamin Boulevard, ph 37 463; and 90 Herzl Street, ph 34 524 — and both are open Sun–Thurs 8am–10pm, Fri 8am–3pm.

Diamimon, 2 Gad Machnes Street, ph 41 725, have the same type of tours, but on a smaller scale. They are open in summer Sun–Fri 8am–10pm, Sat 6–10pm, and winter Sun–Thurs 8am–7.30pm, Fri 10–2pm, Sat 6–7.30pm.

The Abir Brewery have free guided tours, and the opportunity to buy their product at a discount. Take Bus 601 from the Central Bus Station. The brewery opens Sun–Thurs at 10am.

SIGHTSEEING

Netanya is not really a sightseeing town, unless you're really keen on visiting the citrus packing house (which can be organised through the Tourist Information Office). It's a place to relax and soak up the sun, and the beaches are free.

SPORT

We can't let people relax too much, or they won't be fit enough to tackle the rest of the tour around Israel.

Horse Riding

The Ranch, hear Havezelet Ha-Sharon Village, ph 93 655, has riding daily 8am–sunset. Take Bus 17 or 29 from the Central Bus Station.

Cactus Ranch, Itamar Ben-Avi Street, Tobruck, is also open daily 8am–sunset.

Mini-golf

The 18-hole course is on Nice Boulevard, near the Dan Hotel, and is open daily noon–11pm (April–September).

Squash

The Elizur Sports Centre, Radak Street, ph 38 920. Open irregularly, check first. Take Bus 8 from the Central Bus Station.

Tennis

The Elizur Sports Centre — as above.

Maccabi Courts, Ha-Hashmonaim Street, ph 24 054, open Sat–Thurs 8am–10pm, Fri 8am–6pm.

Green Beach Sports Centre, Netanya South, ph 51 466.

Residence Hotel, 18 Gad Machnes Street, ph 33 777 for reservations.

Sailboarding
Kontiki Club on Netanya beach is open daily 8.30am–sunset, and have lessons as well.

Lawn Bowling
The Wingate Institute has greens for the use of visitors, except during the month of May. Ph 96 652 for information.

CAESAREA

The ruins of Caesarea, the Roman capital of Judea, are among Israel's best archaeological sites, and no visitor should miss them. Excavations have revealed a Roman theatre, Byzantine mosaics and aqueducts, a Crusader city, and in the harbour, engineering feats which rival modern technology.

HISTORY
Around 22BC Herod the Great decided to build a city to rival Athens on the site of a 4th century BC Phoenician settlement called Strato's Tower. Herod dedicated it to his benefactor the Roman Emporer Augustus Caesar, and called it Caesarea. Josephus wrote that Strato's Tower was "in a state of decay, but thanks to its admirable situation capable of benefiting by his [Herod's] generosity. He rebuilt it entirely with limestone and adorned it with a most splendid palace. Nowhere did he show more clearly the liveliness of his imagination". Now that was really saying something! Herod may have lacked many things, but imagination wasn't one of them. Josephus goes on to tell of the danger to shipping in the area, then says, "the king by lavish expenditure and unshakable determination won the battle against nature and constructed a harbour bigger than the Piraeus, with further deep roadsteads in its recesses".

The Bible's first mention of Caesarea is in Acts 10 and 11, when St Peter converted to Christianity the Roman centurion, Cornelius. Acts 21:8–14 records St Paul's visit to Caesarea, when he lodged with Philip the evangelist, and Acts 23:23–25 and 25 and 26 tell of his subsequent trials for heresy. The city was by this time

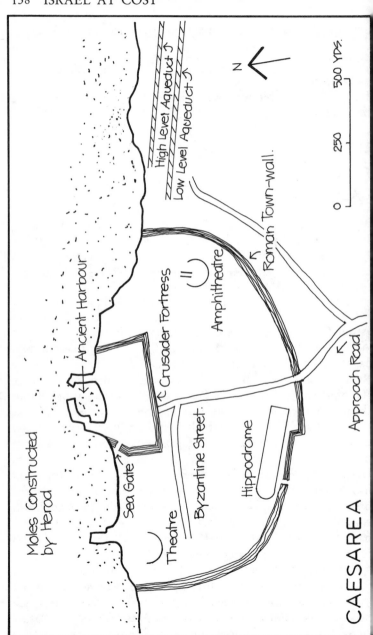

CAESAREA

the headquarters of Roman rule in Israel, and excavations have revealed evidence that Pontius Pilate was the governor from 26 to 36AD — proof, apart from the Biblical record and Josephus' writings, of his actual existence.

The Roman treatment of the Jews led to a revolt in Caesarea in 66BC which started the Jewish Rebellion. The Romans took four years to end the revolt, and celebrated their victory by executing 2500 Jews in the theatre Herod had built in Caesarea. The theatre was also used for the victory celebrations at the end of the Bar Kochba Rebellion, this time with the slow torturing to death of ten Jewish sages, including Rabbi Akiva, the spiritual leader of the Rebellion.

During the 3rd and 4th centuries, Caesarea was a centre of Jewish and Christian learning.

In 640 the Arabs conquered the city, and controlled it until the Crusaders defeated them in 1101. During the Crusades, Caesarea was passed back and forth between the Muslims and the Crusaders, until it was finally captured by King Louis IX of France in 1251. He improved the city's fortifications and built most of the massive ramparts, battlements and the moat which are visible today. But to no avail, for the city was captured by the Mameluke Sultan Baybars in 1265, and destroyed.

In the late 19th century, Muslim refugees from Bosnia, which was soon to become part of Christian Yugoslavia, tried to found a fishing village, but they had a lot of trouble with malaria and decided to head inland and become farmers. In the early 1900s an Arab village was set up, but it was abandoned in 1948.

In 1940 Kibbutz Sedot Yam was established nearby, and when the members commenced to farm the land they came across some of the remains of Caesarea's former glory, leading to many archaeological expeditions, and a programme of restoration.

HOW TO GET THERE

By Bus

Buses run from Tel Aviv, Netanya and Haifa to Hadera approx. every 45 minutes. From here take Bus 76 for Caesarea.

By Car

Caesarea is approx. 55km (34 miles) north of Tel Aviv, and 37km (23 miles) south of Haifa.

ACCOMMODATION

Hotels in Caesarea, and there aren't many of them, are quite expensive and you may be tempted to camp on the beach. Don't. There have been a number of travellers stranded without their money, and often more importantly, their passport.

The prices listed here are for a double room, plus breakfast, per night and are in US Dollars.

Dan Caesarea Golf Hotel, ph (06) 362 266 — $142–152; Mediterranean Nueiba, Michmoret Beach, ph (053) 663 113 — $90; Hofshonit, Kibbutz Sdot-Yam, ph (06) 362 927 — $50.

EATING OUT

Apart from the hotels, the snack bar across from the Crusader city, near the Byzantine Street, has light meals and drinks.

SIGHTSEEING

One ticket (5NIS — half price for children 5–15) allows entry to the Roman Theatre and the Crusader City. The hours are 8am–6pm, 5pm on Fridays and the eves of holidays.

The Roman Theatre

Just inside the gate near the ticket box is a replica of a plaque unearthed during the excavations, which contains the words 'TIBERIVM' and 'TIVS PILATUS', being the reference to Pontius Pilate mentioned in the History section. The original plaque is in the Israel Museum in Jerusalem, which, in my opinion, is ridiculous. The original should be on this site, and the replica in the museum, but unfortunately this sort of thing happens all over the world.

Then there is a short walk to the Roman Theatre. Some will talk about the ampitheatre, but an ampitheatre is circular, and these ruins are semi-circular so the correct term is theatre. There has been some restoration work done here, so many of the seats are not original, but the work has been well done, and it all appears authentic. It is very pleasant to sit on the stone seats, looking at the blue Mediterranean, and letting your imagination run wild. There are many concerts held here, but if there is nothing scheduled when you are in the area, there is always someone willing to go on stage and perform so that you can check out the acoustics.

The Crusader City

Crossing the bridge over the dry moat, it is noticeable that part of the guard tower has toppled into the moat, the work of the Crusaders. Continue on to the gate-house, and take particular note of the old fortifications, the sloping walls and the niches for the archers. Inside the city all the places of interest are well sign-posted in English and Hebrew, but of particular interest are the ruins of the unfinished Crusader Church of St Paul. The Crusaders unknowingly commenced the church on the top of ancient warehouses of Herod's time, and as the construction became larger, and heavier, the whole lot collapsed.

In the main street there are remains of an ancient temple built by Herod and dedicated to Augustus Caesar, and looking out to sea, there are parts of the Crusader port. Underwater excavations have revealed part of Herod's port, and it is possible to join diving tours to explore the depths.

Byzantine Street

Opposite the entrance to the Crusader City and behind the car park and cafeteria, is an excavated Byzantine Street probably from the 2nd and 3rd century. The street is paved with marble and has two interesting statues, one of white marble and the other of red porphyry, both are headless. It is extremely difficult to figure out who the statues represent, obviously, but there are several theories about the lack of heads. It could well be that some new ruler wanted his own statue, and there was a perfectly useful body, so he knocked off the head and stuck on his own. This would have weakened the statue and the head could have fallen off later. Or it could have been that the original subject was not popular, and so the populace took out their dislike on the statues. Or they could have represented some religious characters, which upset members of other sects.

Whatever the reason, there will be no more destruction because the authorities have built a high fence around the street, so you can look, but not touch.

Hippodrome

From the Byzantine Street, about 1km to the east, there is a stone gate in front of a large oval field. This is thought to be the ruins of a hippodrome, most likely built by Herod for his Caesar's Games, and capable of seating 20,000 spectators.

Just past here, on the turn-off to the right, is the only golf course in Israel. It's a very pretty course, with 18 holes, and visitors are welcome.

Aqueduct

When Herod built Caesarea he had one problem — no fresh water. So he built an aqueduct to carry water from the springs at the foot of Mt Carmel to his new city, a distance of 13km (8 miles). At a later stage the Romans doubled its capacity, and while much of the aqueduct remains buried, there is a section visible about 1km north of the Crusader City.

NORTH FROM CAESAREA

Zichron Ya'akov

Zichron Ya'akov was one of the first towns to be settled in Israel, as part of a construction programme due to the involvement of Baron Edmond de Rothschild. His tomb is set among beautiful gardens at Ramat Hanadiv, in between Zichron Ya'akov and another of his towns, Binyamina.

The Carmel winery began operating in Zichron Ya'akov in the late 19th century, and is the main producer of wine in the country. Tours of the winery are available every half hour Sun–Thurs 9am–12.30pm.

Near the wine cellar is the Aaronson Museum, which has exhibits relating to the NILI, an espionage organisation formed during World War I under the leadership of Aaron Aaronson and his family.

Dor

One of the best beaches in Israel, Dor is also an ancient town, probably dating back to the 15th century BC. At the nearby tel there are the ruins of temples dedicated to Zeus and Astarte, and a Byzantine church.

Ein Hod

Ein Hod is an artists' colony 16km (10 miles) south of Haifa. It was started in 1953, and there are now over 60 families living here on the site of an old Arab village, in a semi-cooperative society. The villagers have a council of elders, the workshops are shared, and the art gallery takes a very small commission from sales compared with other galleries. The founder of the colony was

Marcel Yanco, who led the rebuilding of the town. It now has a large gallery, several workshops and an open-air amphitheatre. There is also a reasonably-priced restaurant, and the Yanco-Dada Museum, which has some interesting exhibits.

Aqueduct at Caesarea.

HAIFA

Israel's third-largest city, with a population of approximately 250,000, Haifa is the main port and the industrial centre of the country. It is also the most scenic city, with its Mediterranean coastline and the wooded Mt Carmel.

The city has three levels: the Port in the Old City; the Hadar or business district; and the Carmel district on the summit of Mt Carmel.

There is an old local saying which sums up the city of Haifa — in Jerusalem people study, in Tel Aviv they dance, but in Haifa they work.

HISTORY

Elijah's Mt Carmel victory is well documented in 1 Kings 18:10–40, and 3rd century Talmudic literature makes mention of Mount Carmel and the nearby Jewish village of Sycaminos.

There are different opinions on the origin of the name 'Haifa'. Some say it is from the Hebrew words 'hof yafe' meaning beautiful coast, and others that it comes from the Crusader name 'Cayfe' or 'Caiphas', which was probably from the name of the high priest of Jerusalem during the time of Christ, Caiaphas.

During the Middle Ages, Haifa was a major Arab town, but it was destroyed in a battle with the Crusaders and Akko became more prominent. At the dawn of the 20th century, the population was still only 10,000, and sheep were grazed on the slopes of Mt Carmel.

In 1905 the construction of the Haifa-Damascus Railway began the revival of the city, and then the British completed the modern harbour in 1934, and Haifa was on its way back. Theodor Herzl, the Father of Zionism had visited the city in 1898 and prophesied in his book *Old New Land* that Haifa would have thousands of white houses built on the mountain and huge liners would ride at anchor in the harbour. A visitor to Haifa today will see at once that his prediction has come true.

Haifa was the first city to be controlled by Jews after the end of the British Mandate and the UN decision in 1947.

HOW TO GET THERE

By Air
Air Arkia has flights between Haifa and Eilat, Tel Aviv and Jerusalem.

By Sea
Haifa is the main port of Israel, so most of the cruise ships call in here.

By Bus
There are bus services to and from Jerusalem, Tel Aviv, Akko and Nahariya. The central bus station is on Jaffa Road in Bat Gallim.

By Train
The central railway station is next to the central bus station on Jaffa Road, and trains arrive there from Jerusalem and Tel Aviv.

By Car
Haifa is 159km (99 miles) from Jerusalem and 95km (59 miles) from Tel Aviv.

TOURIST INFORMATION
The main Government Tourist Information Office is at 18 Herzl Street, Hadar, ph 666 521, and there is also an office at Shed 12 (Port) which is only open on the arrival of ships. The hours for the main office are Sun–Thurs 8.30am–5pm, Fri 8.30am–3pm, closed Saturday.

There are Municipal Information Offices at the Central Bus Station, ph 512 208; 23 Hanevi'im Street, Hadar, ph 663 056; and 119 Sederot Hanassi, Central Carmal, ph 383 683.

Haifa Tourism Development Association has its office at 10 Achad Ha'am Street, ph 671 645. It has a very useful pamphlet called 'Haifa At Your Fingertips'.

For recorded information of attractions, phone 640 840 for the programme 'What's on in Haifa'.

ACCOMMODATION
Quite a lot to choose from in Haifa, but here we have given a few examples, with prices for a double room per night, including

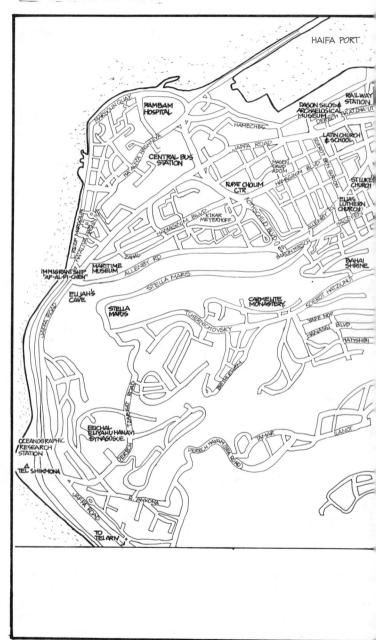

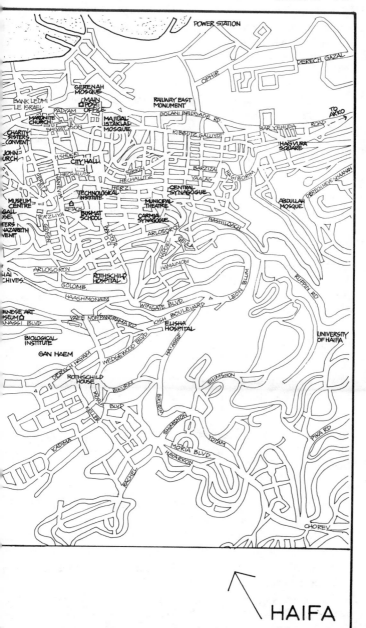

HAIFA

breakfast, in US Dollars, again to be taken only as a guide. T.
Telephone Area Code is 04.

5-star Hotels
Dan Carmel, 87 Hanassi Avenue, ph 386 211 — $122–138; D.
Panorama, 107 Hanasi Avenue, ph 352 222 — $92–102.

4-star Hotels
Nof, 101 Hanassi Avenue, ph 354 311 — $90–100; Shulam
15 Kiryat Sefer Street, ph 342 811 — $68–78.

3-star Hotels
Dvir, 124 Yafe Hof Street, ph 389 131 — $61; Yaarot Hacarm
Mt Carmel, ph 229 144 — $50–66; Carmelia, 35 Herzilya Stre
ph 521 278 — $55; Beth-Shalom Carmel, 110 Hanassi Stre
ph 337 481 — $43.

2-star Hotels
Marom, 51 Hapalmach Street, ph 254 355 — $38; Nesher,
Herzl Street, ph 640 644 — $30–35; Talpiot, 61 Herzl Stre
ph 673 753 — $23–25.

LOCAL TRANSPORT

Bus
There is a good local service run by Egged, which also operates
Saturdays, and buses leave from the Central Bus Station.

Taxi
There are several taxi companies — Neve, ph 222 222; Hamonit
ph 664 343; Carmel, ph 382 727; Carmelit, ph 664 640; Merk
Mitzpa, ph 662 525.

Sherut
These shared taxis link Haifa with other cities in Israel. Differe
companies go to different places:
    To Jerusalem — Aviv, 10 Nordau Street, Hadar, ph 666 33
    To Tel Aviv — Aviv, 10 Nordau Street, Hadar, ph 666 33
    Amal, 157 Jaffa Road, ph 522 828; Arie, 9 Baerwald Stre
        ph 673 666.
    To Acre/Nahariya — Kavei Hagalil, 16 Hanevi'im Stre
        Hadar, ph 664 442; Kikar Plumer, in the port are
        ph 673 666.

Car

ental car companies are — Avis, ph 674 688; Budget, ph 538 558;
urocar, ph 529 504; Hertz, ph 665 425; InterRent, ph 644 069.

ubway

he subway, the only one in Israel, was opened in 1959, and has
cently been renovated. It is only 1800m (1969 yards) long, but
as six stations, beginning at Paris Square in the port area, and
rminating at Gan Ha'Em in Central Carmel. It's a much quicker
ay to get across town than the bus, and is inexpensive.

ATING OUT

elafel stands are everywhere, and Haifa is said to have the best
lafel in Israel. There are also plenty of cafes and coffee shops,
uch as the Bank Cafe, 119 Hanassi Boulevard, Central Carmel,
hich has great cakes, and very reasonably priced meals. Also
ecommended is the Ritz at 5 Haim Street, which is popular with
ocal artists, and even has its own gallery.

For a slightly more expensive meal, try Abu Yousef, 2 Paris
quare, Downtown, ph 663 723, which has good Middle-Eastern
od, or The Cafeteria in the Dan Panorama Hotel, 107 Hanassi
oulevard, ph 352 222, which specialises in seafood.

If you want to splurge there are La Chaumiere, 42A Ben-
Gurion Boulevard, ph 538 563, an exclusive French restaurant; El
Gaucho, 25 Tchernichovsky Street, French Carmel, ph 338 837, an
Argentinian place in the Ahuza Club; Rondi in the Dan Carmel
Hotel, 87 Hanassi Boulevard, ph 386 211; La Trattoria,
19 Hanassi Boulevard, ph 382 020, which, as the name suggests,
as Italian fare.

ENTERTAINMENT

he Tourist Office can provide details of any special events, and of
ourse there are always the hotels, some having live entertainment,
r you can do what the locals do, and go for an evening stroll.

A few bars that are worth mentioning are — Studio 46,
6 Pevsner Street, Ha'okaf, 56 Antwerpen Street in the Dania
Quarter, and London Pride, 85 Ha'atzma'ut Road, which also has
disco.

There are several cinemas, and their programmes are advertised
n the *Jerusalem Post*, and on the recorded 'What's On' service,

ph 640 840. They show American films as well as loc
productions.

The Haifa Municipal Theatre in Hadar, is one of the best t
country has to offer. Most of the performances are in Hebrew. I
on the corner of Pevsner, Yehoshua and Trumpeldor Streets.

The Israel Philharmonic Orchestra performs at the Haifa Aud
torium when it's in town, and when it's not there are usually ope
performances or concerts.

SHOPPING

Jaffa Road is a good place to pick up souvenirs, usually cheap
than elsewhere, and the leading hotels have the usual range
expensive boutiques.

Haifa is well known for its jewellery shops and diamor
dealers, so if you are in the market for these precious stones, go r
further.

There is a branch of Israel's large department store, Hamashb
Lazarchan.

SIGHTSEEING

Baha'i Shrine of the Bab

Set in beautiful gardens in Sderot Hatziunut (Zionism Boulevard
the shrine is the most impressive building that Haifa has to offe
Baha'i is a religion which was developed from a Persian sect calle
Babi, which basically believes that all men are equal, and shoul
love one another. The original leader was The Bab, meaning 'gate
who was martyred in Persia in 1850. His remains were reburied i
this shrine in 1909. Baha'is believe that he was actually a prophe
for he predicted the coming of a man greater than he.

In 1863, a follower, Mizra Husayn Ali, was exiled from Pers
because of his teachings, and declared himself to be the Baha'ulla
(Glory of God), the long-awaited Messiah. It is his teachings th
form the basis of all Baha'i beliefs. In 1868 Baha'ullah was exiled t
Acre by the Turks, and in 1892 he died and was buried in Bahji,
house north of Acre. His tomb is the holiest shrine of the Baha'i fait

The Shrine of the Bab is a mixture of European and Oriental an
is built of Chiampo stone, with columns of Rose Baveno granit
It is open daily 9am–noon, and admission is free, after removin
your shoes. The gardens stay open until 5pm.

Universal House of Justice
Opposite the Baha'i Shrine is a white marble building with Corinthian columns which houses the co-ordinating body of the religion's activities worldwide. The nine-men committee is elected every five years, in a secret ballot, by members of the National Spiritual Assemblies. The building is closed to the public.

Stella Maris (Carmelite Monastery)
The Carmelite order originated in the late 12th century when a group of Crusaders, prompted by the biblical story of Elijah, decided to set up a religious community on the slopes of Mount Carmel. Due to persecution by Muslims, the Carmelites have been forced to move a couple of times, but the present site of the Monastery is believed to be over the cave where Elijah lived. Previously on the site there had been a Greek church, an abbey and a very old chapel, probably from the Byzantine era.

The first monastery the Carmelites built here was used by Napoleon's forces during his campaign of 1799 as a hospital. After the Turks drove him out, they turned on the Carmelites and killed a great many of them. Those that escaped later returned and buried their dead in a pyramid-type garden tomb. Then in 1821 the monastery was partially destroyed by Abdallah, the Pasha of Akko. The present church and monastery, named Stella Maris (Star of the Sea) were opened in 1836, and the remaining old building became a hospice for groups of pilgrims.

There are magnificent paintings in the chapel, and a small museum nearby has some interesting ruins from Byzantine and Crusader periods. Open 8.30am–1.30pm and 3–6pm daily — there is no admission fee.

Around the corner in Tchernichovsky Street is the convent of the Carmelite nuns, which is not open to the public.

Elijah's Cave
There is a track leading from the car park of Stella Maris to a cave that is thought to be the cave where Elijah hid after slaughtering the 450 prophets of Baal (1 Kings 18–19). Why he would hide in this cave when he apparently lived in another cave just up the hill, is beyond me. Anyway, it is also believed that the Holy Family once sheltered here, and as Elijah is acknowledged by Muslims, this cave is holy to the three religions, who come to pray side by side.

The cave is open in summer Sun–Thurs 8am–6pm, Fri 8am–1pm, winter Sun–Thurs 8am–5pm, Fri 9am–1pm, but is always closed on Saturday.

Clandestine Immigration & Navy Museum

Although the name sounds very strange, it sums up this museum very well. It is actually in a boat, the *Af-Al-Pi-Chen*, which was one of many that the Zionists used to illegally immigrate European Jews during the British blockade. The museum is at 204 Allenby Road, ph 536 249, and is open Sun & Thurs 9am–4pm, Mon–Wed 9am–3pm, Fri 9am–1pm, closed Saturday. There is a small admission fee.

National Maritime Museum

With exhibits detailing the history of shipping in the Mediterranean area, and many finds from archaeological expeditions, the Maritime Museum is at 198 Allenby Road, ph 536 622. It is open Sun–Thurs 10am–4pm, Sat 10am–1pm, closed Friday. There is an admission fee, except on Saturday.

Cable Car

There is a cable car running from near Bat Gallim Boulevard, not far from the Central Bus Station, to the Carmelite Monastery. It has a recorded commentary in English and Hebrew, but is quite short and not remarkable. Open Sun–Thurs 9am–11pm, Fri 9am–4pm, Sat 6–11pm.

Dagon Silos & Archaeological Museum

Situated at Pulmer Square on Ha'atzma'ut Street is a different sort of museum. There are free guided tours, at 10.30am Sun–Fri, which tell everything you ever wanted to know about grain — cultivation, storage and distribution. Combined with the tour is a visit to the small archaeological museum, which has some very interesting exhibits.

Haifa Museum

A complex at 26 Shabtai Levi Street, ph 523 325, containing three museums — Museum of Ancient Art, Museum of Modern Art and Museum of Music and Ethnology. They are all open Sun, Mon, Wed 10am–1pm, Tues, Thurs, Sat 10am–1pm and 6–9pm, and there is an admission fee.

Other museums include —

Mane Katz Museum, 89 Yafe Nof Street, ph 83 482, open Sun–Thurs 10am–1pm and 4–6pm, Sat 10am–1pm.

Tikotin Museum of Japanese Art, 89 Hanassi Avenue, ph 383 443, open Sun–Thurs 10am–5pm, Sat 10am–2pm.

Technodea Museum (National Museum of Science and Technology), old Technion Building, between Balfour and Shmaryahu Levin Streets, ph 671 372, open Mon, Wed, Thurs 9am–5pm, Tues 9am–7pm, Fri 9am–1pm, Sat 10am–2pm, closed Sunday.

Railway Museum, old Haifa East Railway Station, ph 531 211, open Sun–Thurs 9am–noon.

Haifa University

The university is worth a visit because from there on the summit of Mount Carmel you can get the best view of Haifa and its surrounds. The modern campus has a 25-storey tower designed by Niemeyer, with a top-floor observatory. There is also the Reuben and Edith Hecht Museum which has a good collection of artifacts relating to Jewish history before the Diaspora. The museum is open Sun–Thurs 10am–1pm, Tues also 4–6pm, Sat 10am–1pm, and free guided tours are given Sun–Thurs at noon, Tues at 5pm and Sat at 11.30am. There are also free guided tours of the campus Sun–Thurs, and information on times will be available on arrival.

Carmel National Park

The fertile southern slopes of Mount Carmel are Israel's largest national park. In ancient times vineyards thrived in the area, and in fact the Hebrew name of Kerem-El means Vineyard of God. It's a great place for picnicking.

Beaches

Bat Gallim is near the Central Bus Station, but is very rocky, and Shaqet beach is close (bus no. 41 from Hadar) but there is a fee to swim at both beaches.

Carmel beach is free, but a bit further away — take bus 44 or 45 from Hadar.

Druze Villages

21km south-east of Haifa, on the Carmel range, is the village of Isfiya, and a few kilometres further on is the village of Daliyat al-Karmel. These are the largest Druze villages in Israel. The Druze speak Arabic, but due to a break with Islam a thousand years ago, they have a secret religion, bordering on Judaism.

While many of the younger people wear western-style clothing, the older wear the traditional outfits. The men have long walrus moustaches, to them a sign of masculinity, and they wear the strangest baggy trousers, with an enormous gusset in the seat. I was told by a local, who seemed to be serious, that the reason for the extra room in the trousers is that Druze believe that the Messiah will be born of a man, so they are ready if they happen to be the chosen one. (I wasn't brave enough to check it out with a Druze.) They also wear the Arabic white scarf on their heads, but it is tied differently and they don't add the black cord. Some men wear a red turban-like headgear, and these are the religious leaders.

The women, who incidentally are quite liberated compared to their Muslim sisters, choose very bright and colourful dresses, and their veils cover only their heads, not their faces.

Isfiya has the remains of a 6th century synagogue, but the people are the main attraction, and Daliyat al-Karmel has a market that is not in any way outstanding, and Beit Oliphant, a former home of Sir Lawrence Oliphant and now a memorial to Druze members of the IDF. Bus nos 92 and 93 run from Haifa to the Druze villages.

Mukhraka

The Carmelite Monastery of Mukhraka is built on the site of Elijah's contest with the priests of Baal (1 Kings 18), and an imposing statue of him stares down somewhat disdainfully at all visitors. The chapel, in keeping with the bible story, has an altar made of twelve stones, and is interesting, but the piece de resistance here is the view. To the east is the Jezreel Valley and the hills of Nazareth, and to the west, the Mediterranean.

TOURS

There is a range of tours on offer by United Tours, 5 Nordau Street, ph 665 656, and Egged Tours, ph 643 131, some for half-day and others full-day. Examples are Caesarea and Tel Aviv, the Druze villages and Megiddo, Nazareth and the Sea of Galilee, Acre and Rosh Hanikra, and the Upper Galilee and Golan. And, of course, there is a city tour.

A free walking tour of the city, organised by the Haifa Tourism Development Association, leaves from a sign-posted point at the corner of Yefe Nof and Sha'ar HaLevenon Streets.

SPORTS

Swimming

Galei Hadar, 9 Hapoel Street, ph 667 854.

Maccabee pool, Bikkurim Street, ph 380 100 (heated in winter).

The Dan Carmel Hotel — pool open to non-residents for 14NIS.

Tennis

The Israel Tennis Centre, Kfar Zamir, ph 522 721.

Maccabee, Bikkurim Street, ph 386 028.

Carmelia, 32 Zionism Boulevard.

City Walls of Akko.

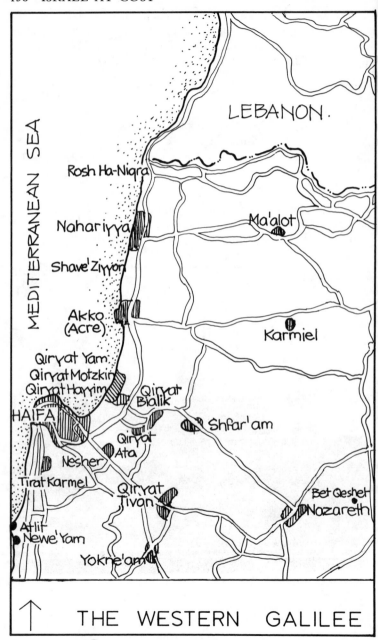

THE WESTERN GALILEE

THE WESTERN GALILEE

ACRE (AKKO)

Acre has one of the best beaches in Israel and is located in the heart of one of the most scenic regions — the Western Galilee and the northern strip of the coast. But it is the Old City of Akko that has become one of Israel's most popular tourist attractions.

HISTORY

Many archaeological expeditions have been carried out in Acre, unearthing one of the oldest settlements in Israel. Papyrus scrolls of the Egyptian Pharaoh Thutmoses III and Rameses II (from the New Kingdom period of Ancient Egypt, 1550–1070BC) which make mention of the city, have been found.

It is thought that the Canaanites settled here about 4000 years ago, and the Bible, in Judges 1:31–32, confirms this with: "Nor did Asher drive out the inhabitants of Akko" but rather settled "among the Canaanites, the inhabitants of the land". Later Akko became part of David's territory (2 Samuel 24:7), but his son Solomon gave it to Hiram, the king of Tyre, in recognition of his help in building the Temple. Hiram, although, evidently wasn't too thrilled with the gift (1 Kings 9:11–14).

Alexander the Great conquered Akko in 332BC, it was renamed Ptolemais, and the population grew to 60,000 causing the city to spread from its early confines of an artificial hill down to the shoreline. It became the largest city-state in Hellenistic Palestine.

Julius Caesar stopped off in Ptolemais in 47BC, and a few years later Herod landed here to start his campaign for the conquest of the Holy Land.

It was from Akko, too, that St Paul embarked on his mission to spread Christianity far and wide.

In 636AD the Arabs took the city, and it reverted to its original name. In 1187 Akko was captured, without much resistance, by Saladin, but four years later along came Richard the Lionheart and Philip of France with the Crusaders who seized the city and changed its name to St Jean d'Acre, or Acre, maybe mistaking it for the Biblical town of Ekron.

After the Crusaders lost Jerusalem in 1192, Acre became the capital of the Crusader Kingdom, but the Mamelukes successfully attacked in 1291 and the city fell. Then followed a period of Ottoman rule, until a Bedouin Sheikh Daher el-Amar captured the town, fortified it and made it his capital. He was defeated by the Turkish Pasha Ahmed el-Jazzar.

In 1799, Napoleon attempted to take Acre, but was defeated by the English fleet, commanded by Sir Sidney Smith.

Ibrahim Pasha, with an Egyptian army, captured Acre from the Turks in 1832 and made it his capital, ruling Palestine and Syria from there for eight years until the Britsh re-installed the Turks. Then Britain captured Palestine in 1917, ousted the Turks, made Haifa their headquarters, and Acre the site of their main prison, in the Citadel.

After the British withdrew in 1948, the Jewish forces captured Acre.

The Old City of Acre visible above ground is only about two centuries old, and seems so peaceful, it is hard to imagine what has gone before.

HOW TO GET THERE

By Bus
There are regular services from Haifa to Nahariya, via Acre, and from Safed to Acre.

By Car
Acre is 22km (14 miles) from Haifa; 117km (73 miles) from Tel Aviv; 45km (28 miles) from Nazareth; and 51km (32 miles) from Safed.

TOURIST INFORMATION

The Government Tourist Information Office is in the Municipality Building, 35 Weizmann Street, ph 910 251, and is open Sun & Wed 7am–12.30pm, 4–6pm, Mon, Tues, Thurs 7am–1.30pm, Fri 7am–12.30pm.

The Municipal Tourist Information Office is at the entrance to the subterranean Crusader City, and is open Sat–Thurs 9am–4.30pm, Fri 9am–12.30pm.

ACCOMMODATION

Because Acre is so close to Haifa, it is more usual to make a day-trip from there, but if you wish to spend longer exploring the sights, here are a few places, with prices for a double room, plus breakfast, per night, in US Dollars, and subject to 15% service charge. The Telephone Area Code is 04.

Palm Beach Club Hotel, Sea Shore, ph 912 891 — $64; Argaman, Sea Shore, ph 916 691 — $48–50; Nes Ammim Guest House, ph 922 566 — $50.

LOCAL TRANSPORT

Because it is only the Old City that you will be interested in, public transport is not necessary. You will be able to reach everything on foot.

EATING OUT

The main street in New Acre, Ben Ami Street, is chock-a-block with the ubiquitous felafel stands and cafes.

The most popular restaurant is on the fishing port, Abu Christo, which predictably serves seafood.

Next door to the el-Jazzar Mosque is the Monte Carlo restaurant, with a large selection of Continental and local dishes. In the market-place, Achim Ouda offers grilled shishkebab and Middle-Eastern salads. For European food, try Zor just outside the Old City walls.

SIGHTSEEING

The following places are set out as for a walking tour commencing along Weizmann Street (Rehov Weizmann).

el-Jazzar's Mosque

The mosque is undoubtedly the most beautiful building in the Old City. Completed in 1781 by Ahmed, an Armenian who was known as el-Jazzar (the butcher) because of his cruelty, the mosque has a rectangular courtyard surrounded on three sides by columns which were brought from ruins at Caesarea and Tyre. The rooms off these arcades were for Muslim pilgrims. The small domed structure in the courtyard contains the remains of el-Jazzar, and his successor, Suleiman Pasha.

The outer and inner walls of the mosque itself are decorated with marble inlays and coloured tiles. Arabic texts are also painted

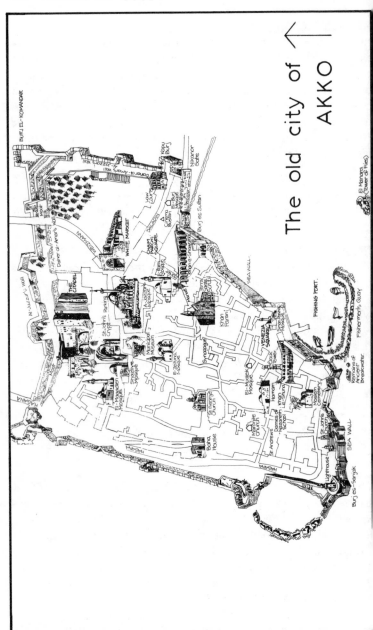

The old city of AKKO

on the inside walls, and as you enter you will see the mihrab, the niche facing south towards Mecca. On the right is the marble pulpit, and above is a gallery for women. In the gallery is a safe which contains what are thought to be hairs from Muhammad's beard.

As at most other places, this was not the original building on this site. First there was a Byzantine church, destroyed by Arabs, then their mosque was destroyed by Crusaders, then their church was destroyed by Arabs — quite a vicious circle.

Subterranean Crusader City

On entering the subterranean city there is a wine press from the Muslim period, which is a bit unusual considering the drinking of wine is forbidden by Islamic law. Then there is a series of chambers with high ceilings called the Knights' Halls. These halls were uncovered by expeditions that began in 1954 and cleared of debris that had filled them for centuries. One hall now houses an exhibition of modern sculpture on a Crusader theme, and another is used for chamber music concerts.

When the Mamelukes finally defeated the Crusaders, they wanted to destroy the city to ensure that other armies could not use its defences. The great size of the buildings made this impossible, so they decided to fill it with rubble, virtually burying it. When el-Jazzar wanted to build his Citadel he chose the spot on top of the Crusader City, unknowingly finishing off the burial. It was not until some Jewish prisoners in the then British held Citadel decided to make their escape through the floors of their cells that the subterranean city was re-discovered. In a passage outside the Knights' Halls there is a concrete patch in the ceiling covering the prisoners' escape efforts.

Crusader St Jean d'Acre housed a number of religious orders, and each had their own self-contained quarters. The largest belonged to the Order of St John, called the Hospitallers, which were originally founded, as the name suggests, to provide hospital care for ailing pilgrims, but became more of an armed protection unit and a major part of the Crusader Kingdom's defence.

The largest and most awe-inspiring underground room is the inaptly named Crypt of St John, which was really the dining hall of the knights. As it is known that Marco Polo stopped off in Acre on his was to the Orient, he was probably wined and dined in this room. The 12m-high vaulted ceiling is supported by three gigantic columns with carvings of the fleur-de-lys, the earliest known use of the French emblem. Next to the last column is a 60m underground passage which leads to the rooms and courtyard of the Crusaders' hospital. The Turks used this part as a post office, so it is also known as The Post (Al-Bosta).

There is an exit from the underground city just near here.

The Crusader City is open Sat–Thurs 9am–4.30pm, Fri 9am–12.30pm. There is an admission fee, which also includes the Municipal Museum.

Municipal Museum

Until 1948, the building that houses the museum was a public bathhouse, with steam rooms and cold pools, as was intended by its original builder in 1780, Ahmed el-Jazzar. It was decided to use it as a museum in 1953, and while renovations were taking place, remains of Roman and Crusader hot water installations were found beneath the site.

Now there is a permanent folklore exhibition of rural Arab and Druze villages and displays of archaeological finds.

The Markets

Acre is no longer an important centre, but like every other eastern city it has its market, though somewhat small. The two-century old Souk el-Abayd (White Bazaar) is typical in its design, a narrow street lined by shops on each side.

In recent years archaeologists have discovered another Souk which had been filled in. It has now been restored.

The Khans

On the south-eastern side of old Akko there are three caravanserais or 'khans'. A caravanserai, by the way, was a way-station for the old horse and camel caravans.

The Khan e-Shawarda is very dilapidated, though it is still possible to see the remains of the colonnades, and to imagine how they must have been.

Next to the Terra Santa School is the Khan el-Faranj, the Khan of the Franks. In the Crusader period this was the centre of the merchants of Venice, the Venetian Inn.

Khan el-Umdan, the Inn of the Columns, is the most attractive the three khans. It is surrounded by two-storeyed buildings with colonnades, the ground floor being used for the animals, and the upper floor for the people. It also has a tall Turkish clock tower, one of Acre's main landmarks.

Fishing Port

Near the Khan el-Umdan is the fishing port, with boats waiting to take you for a trip for a view of the city from the outside. Don't take the first price they offer.

During the Crusader period there would have been as many as 1000 ships anchored in the inner and outer harbour, which is difficult to envisage with what is there today.

Acre was the only port along the Palestinian coast that offered shelter from storms, being protected on three sides by land, and on the fourth by a breakwater. The Persians were the first to develop Acre as a major port in the 6th century BC. The Arabs enlarged the harbour in the 9th century BC, and made an inner harbour sealed off at night by a chain across its narrow entrance. The Tower of Flies, part of which can be seen today, was strongly fortified and guarded access to the harbour.

The harbour is now only accessible to small ships, being largely choked with sand, and Haifa has become the major port. To add insult to injury, the Bay between the two cities which for thousands of years had been the Bay of Acre, is now called the Bay of Haifa.

The Citadel

Built by el-Jazzar two centuries ago, the Citadel was supposed to survive even if the rest of the city fell. The central wing is called the Tower of the Treasury, where originally el-Jazzar locked up his loot, and later where the British locked up political prisoners.

In 1947, members of the Jewish underground staged a spectacular raid on the prison allowing more than 200 prisoners to escape, although nearly a dozen of the liberators were killed.

Today the Citadel houses the Hall of Heroism, a small museum dedicated to Jewish underground movements during the British mandate. The museum is open Sat–Thurs 9am–5pm, Fri 9am–12.30pm and there is an admission fee.

At the north-western corner, where the sea wall meets the land wall, is Burj Kuraijim, and from here the moat and al-Jazzar's wall lead to the bus station.

Modern Acre

After the War of Liberation, and the resultant growth in immigration, the city of Acre began stretching northward along the Bay. It now has a population of approximately 35,000.

The ancient city had been a centre for glassmaking (many believe that the art of making glass originated here) and dyeing, but the modern city is an industrial centre with steel plants, textile mills and other factories.

Acre is also a holiday resort because of its beaches, notably Purple Beach, so called because the snails that once frequented the area were used to make a purple dye. Even though it does charge an entrance fee, the beach is very popular.

The Baha'i Shrine

The tomb of Baba'u'llah, the holiest shrine of the Baha'i faith, is situated just outside Acre, on Bus no. 271 route. Siyyid Ali Mohammed was born in Shiraz, Persia in 1819, and at the age of 25 delivered his Declaration — "I am the Bab, the Gate to a new age of Peace and Universal Brotherhood". Of course, not everyone agreed with him, so he was arrested and executed six years later. The spread of the new faith was taken up by Mirza Husseyn Ali, a Persian nobleman, who called himself the Baba'u'llah, 'Glory to God'. He was not completely believed either, and wound up imprisoned in Acre's citadel. On his release he lived in a mansion, Bahje House, in whose gardens is his tomb. The house is now a museum and is open Fri–Sun 9am–noon, with no admission charge. The gardens are open daily 9am–5pm.

NAHARIYA

Nahariya was established in 1934 by German Jews who had escaped Nazism, and were determined to live their lives in safety on their new farms. They were not really cut out for an agricultural life-style, so they turned their attention to the town's other natural resource, the beach. The tourist industry started with families taking visitors into their homes as paying guests, and like Topsy it just grew, becoming very popular especially with honeyooners. The town now has a population of over 30,000, but anages to retain its small town atmosphere.

IOW TO GET THERE

y Bus
here are services from Akko and Haifa, approximately every 0 minutes.

y Train
somewhat unreliable service between Haifa and Nahariya.

y Car
Nahariya is approximately 35km (22 miles) from Haifa, and 10km miles) from Acre.

OURIST INFORMATION
he office of the Israel Government Tourist Office is in the Egged us Station, Sederot Ga'ton, ph 922 121.

ACCOMMODATION
s mentioned above, Nahariya is a tourist town, so finding ccommodation is not a problem. Here are a few examples, with rices for a double room, including breakfast, in US Dollars, and ibject to a 15% service charge. They should be used as a guide nly. The Telephone Area Code is 04.

-star Hotels
Carlton, 23 Ha'gaaton Boulevard, ph 922 211 — $80; Pallas thene, 28 Hamaapilim Street, ph 922 381 — $63–70.

-star Hotels
den, Meyasdim Street, ph 923 246 — $52–58; Frank, 4 Haaliya treet, ph 920 278 — $50–56; Panorama, 6 Hamaapilim Street, h 920 555 — $50; Rosenblatt, 59 Weizman Street, ph 923 469 — 45; Astar, 27 Gaaton Boulevard, ph 923 431 — $45; Yarden, 8 Hameyasdim Street, ph 922 966 — $35–50; Kalman, 7 Jabotinsky Street, ph 920 355 — $35–45.

-star Hotels
rna, 29 Jabotinsky Street, ph 920 170 — $35; Karl Laufer, 1 Hameyasdim Street, ph 92 130.

LOCAL TRANSPORT

There is a local bus service, but it's not very reliable. The beac
and most hotels are within walking distance of the bus and trai
stations, and for trips further afield most people seem to hire
bicycle from the Youth Hostel.

You can also travel by horse and cart, which is a bit expensiv
and definitely not for animal lovers.

EATING OUT

The main street, Sederot Ga'aton (or if you prefer HaGa'ato
Boulevard) has restaurants and coffee shops from one end to th
other, but apart from the Donau at no. 32, ph 923 956, with i
Romanian menu, they are nothing to rave about.

There are two good Chinese restaurants, the Chinese In
Restaurant, 28 HaGa'aton (enter from the rear) and the Singapo
Chinese Garden, corner of Jabotinsky and Mayasdim.

SIGHTSEEING

Beaches

The main beach is Galei Gallil, reached by following HaGa'ato
Boulevard to its western end. There is an admission fee to th
beach, which has a swimming pool as well.

To the north and south are stretches of good, free beaches

Temple Ruins

North of Galei Gallil are the ruins of a Phoenician or Canaanit
temple dating from the 18th or 17th century BC. It was apparentl
dedicted to Astarte, goddess of the sea, and of love and fertility
Some claim that a spring nearby promotes fertility.

Museum

In the Municipality building there is a small museum with exhibi
of local archaeological finds, but it is not very exciting. Ope
Sun–Fri, 10am–noon, Sun & Wed 4–6pm, and there is n
admission fee.

Achziv

About 5km (3 miles) north of Nahariya is Achziv, which was a
ancient Canaanite city assigned to the tribe of Asher. The Phoen
cians also established a port here, and remains have been foun
from the Bronze Age. But the most noticeable thing in the area i

the Club Mediterranee, which has a public beach adjacent to it, built to placate the locals.

The tel of ancient Achziv, to the north of the Club, has become a national park, but few of its ancient buildings remain.

Rosh Hanikra

Rosh Hanikra is the end of Route 4, on the border with Lebanon, where the mountain ridge descends to the sea. There was no way through the mountains in ancient times to the lands of the Phoenicians, and the climb up and over was called the Ladder of Tyre. In 1943, New Zealand army engineers built a railway line through the hills to extend the Cairo-Tel Aviv-Haifa line to Beirut, but all that is left now is a dirt road.

The major attractions here are the caves which have been carved by the sea at the bottom of the cliffs. They have been favourably compared with those at Capri, and can be reached by a cable car. Some people do swim into the caves, but it is not recommended, firstly because of the extremely strong currents, and secondly because this is a border with armed guards, and the border line extending out into the water is hard to judge. For the same reason, it is wise not to be snap-happy with cameras. The cable car runs Sat-Thurs 8.30am-6pm, Fri 8.30am–4pm, and is quite expensive.

Border at Metulla.

The UPPER GALILEE and The GOLAN

UPPER GALILEE AND THE GOLAN

Undoubtedly one of the greenest parts of Israel, the area can be divided into three:

The Highlands (Merom Hagalil) — a range of mountains from the Mediterranean coast, running along the border with Lebanon and reaching into Lower Galilee in the south and Hula Valley in the east.

The Hula Valley — a long, cultivated valley, with many modern agricultural settlements. The northern end of the valley sees the three main tributaries of the Jordan unite and flow towards the Sea of Galilee.

The Golan and the slopes of Mount Hermon — a volcanic area, with Israel's only ski resort. The Golan is roughly semi-circular in shape and is 60km (38miles) from north to south, and about 25km (16 miles) at its widest point. After World War I it was part of Syria and under French control, but it was during Israel's War of Independence in 1948 that the Golan became a battlefield. There are well-marked Syrian bunkers you can visit, BUT be careful not to wander outside the marked fences as there are still undetonated mines in the area, and people have been injured, and even killed, due to indiscriminate curiosity.

Three parallel roads approach the Upper Galilee from the west coast, Route 85 from Acre, Route 89 from Nahariya, and a road further north from Shlomi.

MA'ALOT

Built in 1957 to cater for the influx of Jewish refugees from Arab lands, Ma'alot is 18km (11 miles) east of Nahariya. It is not a tourist town, but as you drive through it, the name may ring a bell. It was here in May 1974 that a PLO terrorist group captured a school and held hostage a group of high-school children on an excursion from Safed. A rescue attempt failed, and the terrorists shot and killed 24 of the children. All may not have been forgiven, but the town now has a common local council with the neighbouring Arab town of Tarshiha.

PEKI'IN

Peki'in is on the road which links Route 89 to Route 85, the Acre-Safed road, and is a Druze-Arab village. But it has had a continuous Jewish presence for 2000 years according to tradition so these people were never exiled from the Holy Land. Most of the Jews had left the village by the late 1930s, but the old synagogue built on the site of several more ancient, is worth visiting. Near the village is a small cave which is believed to be where Shimon Bar Yochai, a rabbi of the 2nd century, and his son, Eliezer, hid from the Romans for 13 years to escape a law which made the study of the Torah illegal. Legend says that they lived on spring water and the bean of the carob tree. The cave is a sacred site to Jews.

BAR'AM

East of Ma'alot at the Sasa road intersection, there is a mountain road leading off to the left to the ancient synagogue remains of Bar'am. These remains are very well preserved, probably the best preserved in Israel.

MOUNT MERON

The highest mountain in the Galilee, and the second highest in Israel, at 1208m (3,926 ft), Mount Meron's slopes are Israel's largest nature reserve (10,100ha–25,000 acres). There is a good road almost to the top of the mountain, and a walking trail encircles the peak. The slopes were inhabited in the Old Testament times and the late Roman period, but today the animals, such as polecat and wild boar, are the sole occupants. Formerly leopard and antelope roamed the area, but they are now extinct.

At the eastern foot of Mount Meron there are tombs of several great rabbis of the Roman period, such as Hillel, the sage of the Herodian period, and his contemporary Shammai, but more revered is the tomb of Shimon Bar-Yochai, survivor of the Bar Kochba Revolt.

SAFED

Safed is Israel's highest city at 900m (3,000 ft). It is a very old city, and has a great many Hasidim Jews. These people are Orthodox, and the men wear long black coats, white shirts, ill-fitting big black hats, and long side curls (payot). The payot are the result of one of the laws that the Lord gave to Moses: "You shall not shave around the sides of your head, nor shall you disfigure the edges of your beard." (Leviticus 19:27) Other commandments in the same Book explain the friendly manner of these people: "And if a stranger sojourns with you in your land, you shall not mistreat him" (19:33). "But the stranger who dwells among you shall be to you as one born among you, and you shall love him as yourself" (19:34).

The city is very peaceful, and has a maze of cobbled streets — a very picturesque place.

HISTORY

After Joshua conquered the land of Israel, the Lord commanded him to divide it between the tribes of Israel, and Safed was part of that given to the children of Naphtali (Joshua 19:32–39). Old Safed was built on a hill called the Citadel, and during the First Temple period, it, like many other hill-top towns, lit masu'ot or beacons to signify the beginning of a new month, or a holy day.

Safed was one of the towns fortified by Josephus Flavius, then general of the Jewish forces in Galilee, during the First Revolt (66–73AD). He says in *The Jewish War* that he "directed the work and himself lent a hand".

The 2nd century saw the beginning of Kabbalism, or Jewish mysticism, in Safed when Rabbi Shimon Bar Yochai 'received' a book of Jewish mystical teachings, the Zohar (Book of Splendour). The word 'Kabbalah' is derived from the Hebrew word for 'to receive'. The Kabbalists wanted to find out exactly what God wanted them to do so that they could live their lives in complete holiness.

During the Middle Ages, the Crusaders built a powerful fortress which was captured by Saladin in 1188, but regained and refurbished in 1238 by the Order of the Templars, who made it the largest Christian fortress in the East. But it couldn't resist the force of the Marmelukes who took it in 1266.

Meanwhile the Jewish community continued to grow, and reached its zenith in the 16th century due to an influx of Kabbalists deported from Spain during the Spanish Inquisition. Safed became the world centre of Jewish learning.

The town then had a series of natural disasters — a plague in 1742, an earthquake in 1769, and another in 1837 — and most of the survivors left. By 1948, the large Jewish majority of the 1800s no longer existed. When the British army withdrew, Safed's main strategic positions were left to the Arabs, who took steps to drive out the remaining (couple of thousand) Jews who were in the main elderly. In a real turn around, which has come to be called 'The Miracel of Safed', the Jews survived and managed to drive out the Arabs.

With the creation of the State of Israel, Safed's population was bolstered by an increase in religious Jews, and Jewish artists. Both were attracted by the peaceful surroundings and temperate climate. It also became a popular summer tourist spot, but this has declined since the Sea of Galilee has become more accessible.

HOW TO GET THERE

By Bus
There are services to Safed from Tiberias, Haifa, Acre, Tel Aviv and Jerusalem.

By Road
Safed is 36km (22 miles) from Tiberias; 72km (45 miles) from Haifa; 51km (32 miles) from Acre; 168km (104 miles) from Tel Aviv; and 192km (119 miles) from Jerusalem.

TOURIST INFORMATION
The Israeli Government Tourist Office is at 23 Jerusalem Street, ph 930 633, open Sun–Thurs 8.30am–12.45pm, 4–6pm, Fri 9am–1pm.

ACCOMMODATION
Here are some examples, with prices for a double room plus breakfast per night in US Dollars, which should be used as a guide only. The Telephone Area Code is 06.

4-star Hotel
Rimon Inn, Artists' Colonym, ph 930 665 — $75.

3-star Hotels
Ron, Hativat Yiftah Street, ph 972 590 — $72; Pisgah, Mt Canaan, ph 930 105 — $46; Zefat, Mt Canaan, ph 930 914 — $46; Ruckenstein, Mt Canaan, ph 930 060 — $45; David, Mt Canaan, ph 930 062 — $41; Nof Hagalil, Mt Canaan, ph 931 595 — $40; Tzameret Canaan, POB 155, ph 930 157 — $37.

LOCAL TRANSPORT
There are no great distances involved in seeing all the sights, so transport is not necessary.

EATING OUT
Safed is not the gourmet capital of the world, but it's not the food that brings travellers here. There are, of course, felafel bars, and Universal Felafel, 54 Jerusalem Street, is probably the best.

Also on Jerusalem Street: The Hotel Beit Yosef, at no. 2, has a buffet menu that is quite good; the Cafe California has reasonably priced snacks; Pinati offers reasonable Middle-Eastern food; Batia, has Oriental/European cuisine; and Hamifgash has Kosher dishes.

In the artists' quarter the most popular eating, and meeting, place is Milo.

SIGHTSEEING
The Citadel (Gan HaMetsuda)
On the summit of Mount Safed is the Citadel, where the beacons were lit in early times, and where Josephus built his defensive structures. The ruins that are visible today, though, are those of the Crusader fortress, and in fact, Jerusalem Street, the main thoroughfare of Safed, skirts the outline of the Crusader city wall. Archaeological excavations in 1986 discovered pieces of pottery from the time of Abraham, and more digs are planned in the area.

The view from the Citadel is extremely good, and on a clear day you can see the Sea of Galilee. The trees around Safed have been planted by the Jewish National Fund, who have been very busy planting trees all over Israel. Part of the pride that the Jews have in their homeland is their wish to make it a green country. For about 8NIS the Fund plants a sapling and presents you with a certificate of ownership, and it has become popular for these to be given as presents for birthdays, etc. The fact that you never actually see the trees, or even know where they are planted, doesn't seem to worry anybody, and it has to be admitted that the system is working, Israel is becoming a green place.

The Jewish Quarter
The major attraction of Safed, the Jewish Quarter, has its centre at Kikar HaMaginim (Defenders' Square), or as it is commonly known, the Kikar. HaMaginim Street leads to it from Jerusalem Street.

The synagogues are open to visitors throughout the day, and there is no entrance fee, but donations are expected. Of course, suitable clothing must be worn, and men must wear a yarmulka (skull cap) — cardboard yarmulkas are available near the entrance.

Ha'Ari Ashkenazi Synagogue — one of two synagogues dedicated to Rabbi Itzhak Luria, the 'Ari'. He was born in Jerusalem in 1534, but it was in Cairo that he studied Kabbalah. He moved to Safed in 1569 so he could learn more from the leading teacher of mysticism, Rabbi Moshe Cordeviero. After the death of Cordeviero, Rabbi Itzhak took over as head teacher. The Synagogue was built after his death.

Be very careful if you walk into a small room at the back of the synagogue. There is a carved chair known as Elijah's Chair, and it is believed that couples who sit in it are guaranteed to have a son within a year.

Caro Synagogue — stands on the site of the home of Rabbi Yosef Caro, who was once the chief rabbi in Safed. Born in Spain in 1488, he fled to the Balkans in 1492, and moved to Safed in 1535. His claim to fame is the *Shulchan Aruch* a series of works detailing how to live a perfect Jewish life.

The synagogue was destroyed by earthquake in 1837 and rebuilt in 1847, and the ark contains some very interesting scrolls, which with permission, visitors can view.

Alsheikh Synagogue — named after another leading Kabbalist, Rabbi Moses Alsheikh. Of note near here are the houses which are all painted blue, the colour of heaven.

Abuhav Synagogue — built in the 1490s by followers of Rabbi Yitzhak Abohav. The synagogue has four central pillars, representing earth, water, air and fire, which Kabbalists believe make up creation; the dome has ten windows, representing the Commandments; pictures of the twelve tribes of Israel, representing Jewish unity; illustrations of the Dome of the Rock, signifying the Temple's destruction.

Banni Synagogue — named after Rabbi Yossi Banni, and also known as the Shrine of the White Saint. Rabbi Banni is buried here, and the other name comes from a legend in which he apparently changed black chickens to white when an Arab governor decreed that only white chickens could be used for the Yom Kippur ceremony.

Ha'Ari Sephardic Synagogue — where Rabbi Itzhak Luria, with the prophet Elijah, learned the mystical texts.

Cemeteries

On the western slopes below the Old City are two cemeteries. The oldest is where the bodies of the famous Kabbalists are interred, including Itzhak Luria, Moshe Cordoviero, Yossi Banni, Yosef Caro and Ya'acov Beirav.

The body of the prophet Hosea is believed by the Karaites of Damascus to be buried in the domed tomb nearby. Some also believe that Hannah and her seven sons who were martyred by the Greeks at the beginning of the Maccabean revolt are buried on the hill.

The newer cemetery has many victims from the 1948 siege, and in a separate plot the bodies of the teenagers killed by the terrorists at Ma'alot in 1974.

Hameira House

In the House, which dates from 1517, there are a museum, a research institute and the centre for educational tourism. The building has had a turbulent history having been destroyed by earthquakes, and wars over the years, but it was restored between 1959 and 1984 by Yehzkel Hameiri, a fifth generation Safedian.

The Museum's exhibits show the lifestyles of previous generations, and are aimed at making visitors understand the Jewish community. Open Sun–Fri 9am–2pm.

The Research Institute documents the history of Safed's Jewish community.

The Centre for Educational Tourism has classrooms and a lecture hall which can be hired for tour groups and seminars. They can arrange lecturers and accommodation. For information ph 971 307.

Ma'alot Olei HaGardom Street
Built by the British after the 1929 Arab riots, Ma'alot Olei HaGardom Street (Hebrew for Men Who Were Hungry) is a wide stairway that separates the Jewish Quarter from the Artists Quarter. From the top of the stairs can be seen the ruins of 16th century houses built out of stones from the Crusader wall. Also visible, looking towards Gan HaMetsuda, is the bullet-ridden former British police station, and a British gun position on the roof of a building.

Artists' Quarter
What was once called the Arab Quarter is now home to painters, potters, sculptors and their galleries. If this is your reason for visiting Safed, allow about 5 hours to see everything, and make sure it is summer as many of the artists winter in warmer regions. am not going to attempt to recommend any particular galleries as things can change, but you won't have any trouble finding them.

Zvi Assaf Printing Museum
It was in Safed that the first printing press in the country was set up, and the first book in Hebrew was printed in 1578. The Printing Museum, off Rimonim Street, has many exhibits and is open Sun–Thurs 10am–noon, 4–6pm, Fri–Sat 10am–noon, and there is no entrance fee.

TOURS
Egged Tours, at the Central Bus Station, have tours to the local religious sites and to outlying centres.

There is a walking tour run by Shlomo Bar-Ayal, who can be contacted through the Hotel Beit Yosef, ph 930 012. The two hour tour gives an insight into this town of Jewish mysticism, and in summer he runs three tours Sun–Thurs at 9.30am, 1pm and 4pm, Fri one tour at 9.30am. In winter Sun–Fri there is one tour only at 10.30am.

ROSH PINNA

Rosh Pinna means 'cornerstone' and it was given its name by the Romanian Jews who established a farming community here in the late 1880s.

The town is at the junction of roads from Haifa, Akko, Safed and Tiberias, so this is where bus travellers usually have to change vehicles.

HATZOR

Situated on the road leading from Rosh Pinna to Metulla on the Lebanese border, Hatzor has a rich history. It was mentioned frequently in Egyptian and Assyrian records as early as the 19th century BC. The Bible tells that Josuha, during his campaign to regain the land for the children of Israel, "took Hazor, and struck its king with the sword; for Hazor was formerly the head of all those kingdoms". He then promptly burned it to the ground (Joshua 11:10–11).

There is no doubt that it had been a large city for archaeologists working on the tel of the ancient city say that its area was about 85ha (210 acres) — about three times larger than the next biggest, Tel Dan.

The Book of Joshua goes on to say that Hazor became part of the inheritance of the tribe of the children of Judah (15:20–25), but the city did not regain its importance until Solomon rebuilt it, along with Megiddo and Gezer (1 Kings 9:15). It was finally conquered by Tiglath-Pileser, King of Assyria, and the inhabitants taken as slaves (2 Kings 15:29), and never became more than a small town again.

Archaeologists, led by Yigael Yadin who worked at Masada, began digging in 1955, and uncovered twenty-one different strata of settlement. The earliest was dated at the Early Bronze Age and the latest at the Hellenistic period.

Visitors may wander around the tel, but to get a background of what there is to see, it is best to first visit the museum opposite. Open Sun–Thurs 8am–4pm, Fri 8am–1pm, and there is an admission fee.

HULA VALLEY

The Hula Valley is lush and green today, but this was not always the case. It was originally a very large swamp surrounding Lake Hula. At the turn of the century settlers moved into the area, but were virtually plagued by malaria. Incidentally, the word 'malaria' means 'bad air' which people thought caused the disease before the dreaded mosquito was found to be the culprit. Anyway, realising that underneath the lake and surrounding swamp there was rich arable land, the Israelis undertook an engineering project to drain them and reclaim the land.

This was going to interfere with the animal, bird and plant life, so in stepped the 'greenies' in the form of the Society for the Protection of Nature in Israel. And, amazingly in this type of conflict, a compromise was reached. They all decided to leave a portion of the swamp as a wetlands reserve and wildlife sanctuary. It is called the Hula Nature Reserve. It is open to visitors Sat–Thurs 8am–4pm, Fri 8am–3pm, and there is an admission fee. There are also free guided tours on Sat, Sun, Tues and Thurs between 9.30am and 1.30pm.

Unfortunately, if you are travelling by bus from Rosh Pinna to Kiryat Shmona, the closest stop is about 2.5km from the reserve entrance.

KIRYAT SHMONA

The name Kiryat Shmona means 'the Town of the Eight', and refers to the eight people who lost their lives in defence of Tel Hai in 1920. The town is basically the service centre for the surrounding farmlands, and has been the target of many Arab terrorist attacks. It really doesn't have much to offer as far as sightseeing goes.

TEL HAI

The site of the heroic stand mentioned above, Tel Hai has a special place in Israeli history. After World War I, France and Great Britain had many discussions over which one should have control of the upper Hula Valley, as it bordered the territory of each nation. Meanwhile the Bedouins and Arabs made life a hell or

rth for the small Jewish settlements, whose pleas for help fell on
af ears.

The defence of Tel Hai not only brought attention to their
ight, it also was the first time in the modern era that Jews armed
emselves and fought, changing their reputation from being
fenceless and timid.

When the League of Nations drew the final borders for the
ritish mandated territory of Palestine in 1922, the upper Hula
alley was included, and as a result also included in the State of
rael after 1948.

The watchtower of the original settlement has been fitted out as
museum. It is open in winter Sun–Thurs 8am–4pm, Fri
m–1pm, Sat 9am–2.30pm, and in summer Sun–Thurs
m–1pm, 2–5pm. There is an admission fee.

ETULLA

etulla is the most northern settlement in Israel, and is situated on
e border with Lebanon. It was founded as a village of indepen-
nt farmers in 1896 through a grant from Baron Edmond de
othschild, and has prospered as an agricultural and bee-keeping
llage. It has a barbed-wire fence at the border which is known to
e Israelis as the 'Good Fence', but no-one says what the
ebanese call it. Apparently Lebanese workers are allowed
rough the border checkpoint to work on the Jewish farms.

There is a strong military presence here, but the soldiers seem to
much more interested in having their photographs taken with
e tourists than keeping an eye on the fence, or maybe I was there
hen they were changing shifts. There is also a good souvenir
op and snack bar, and a cairn showing the flags of both
untries, with dozens of people lined up to have their photo-
aphs taken holding onto both flag poles.

Looking across the border into Lebanon it is possible to see
eaufort Castle, originally a Crusader fortress, but more recently
ed by the PLO.

AHAL IYON NATURE RESERVE

e park is not a year-round attraction as the waterfalls dry up in
mmer, so it is best visited in spring or late winter. Nahal Iyon is

a small canyon with good walking tracks and four waterfalls. T
lowest and best is the Tannur waterfall, which means 'oven'
some say because of the shape of the rock formation; oth
because the spray from the falls resembles steam from an ove
The entrance to the park is between Tel Hai and Metulla, and t
bus stops nearby.

North of the Tannur is the tel of the ancient city of Abel of Be
Maachah, the refuge of Sheba from David (2 Samuel 20:1–2.

TEL DAN

The Bible tells that the children of Dan captured the city
Leshem, changed its name to Dan and added it to the lot giv
them after Joshua's conquest (Joshua 19:40–48). The tel is t
second largest discovered, giving some idea of its importance
ancient times. The Book of Judges, and both Books of Samuel u
the expression 'from Dan to Beersheba' to denote the extent of t
Promised Land in that time. And in 1 Kings 12:27–30, wh
Jeroboam was trying to turn the people against the house of Dav
and stop them going to the Temple in Jerusalem, it was at Dan tl
he set up one of his golden calves. Excavations have revealed alt
from this period.

The local Arabs have another name the for site — Tel el-Ka
the Hill of the Judge. Legend has it that the three rivers in the ar
the Dan, the Banias and the Hatzbani, continually argued o
which was the mightiest of the three. Eventually they asked G
to come down and settle the question once and for all. He arriv
and sitting on the hill, told them to unite and become one stro
river. They did — and we call it the Jordan.

A short bus ride from here is Kibbutz Dan and the B
Ussishkin Museum with exhibits on local flora, fauna and histo
Open Sun–Thurs 9am–noon, 1–3pm, Fri 9am–12.30pm,
10am–2pm.

BANIAS

We have now entered the Golan area, and a few kilometres furtl
on this road is Banias, called by the ancient Greeks 'Panias'. Th
is a large cave which was a cult centre for the worship of the g

an, god of shepherds and forests, and in the cliff face there are the
emains of several niches which would have held statues of Pan.

A natural spring rushes out of a hole beneath the cave, the water
riginating from the slopes of Mt Hermon, and going on to be one
f the main sources of the River Jordan.

After changing hands a couple of times, the town was given by
1e Roman emperor to Herod the Great who built a temple
edicated to Augustus Ceasar. When Herod died the town passed
o his son, Philip, who built it into a city and changed its name to
Caesarea Philippi. It was to this city that Jesus went with his
isciples and asked, "Who do men say that I, the Son of Man,
m?" and later said to Simon, "You are Peter, and on this rock I
vill build my church" (Matthew 16:13-20). There are scholars
vho believe that Caesarea Philippi was especially chosen for these
vents because it was the main paganistic centre of the time.

During the Crusader period a town was built here to defend the
oad between Damascus and Tyre. There are some ruins of this,
•ut not much remains of earlier periods.

North of Banias, off Route 99, there is a Syrian bunker which
vill give you an idea of the strategic value of the Golan Heights.
When driving through the Golan it is very easy to pick out the
ites of many Syrian bunkers, because of the ingenuity of an Israeli
ntelligence Officer, by the name of Cohen. He infiltrated the
•yrian hierarchy and managed to convince them that the bunkers
1eeded more shade for the men who might have to stay in them for
ong periods of time. The answer was to plant quick-growing trees
lose to the bunkers, and gum trees were chosen. Of course, they
tuck out among the native flora like the proverbial sore finger,
•nabling the Israeli Army to locate and destroy the bunkers. By
he way, this is not an invitation for you to explore every gum tree
hat you see, THERE ARE UNDETONATED LAND MINES
N THE AREA.

NIMROD CASTLE

North of Banias, Route 989 veers to the left to Nimrod's Castle,
he best preserved Crusader castle in Israel. Why the name
Nimrod? Well, nobody knows for sure, but legend says that the
Biblical Nimrod (Genesis 10:8-10) built the first castle on this site.
There doesn't seem much evidence to back this up, though.

What is known is that the castle that we see today was built b
the Crusader Baldwin II in 1129 to protect against attack fro
Damascus, but the Damascenes were victorious in 1132, only to b
defeated by Arabs in 1137. Then it was passed back and fort
between Arabs and Crusaders, became the possession of th
Mamelukes for a while, used as a political prison, then abandone

During the Six Day War, it was first used by the Syrians an
then by the Israelis, but neither seems to have done much damag
to the castle remains. Open Sat–Thurs 8am–5pm, Fri 8am–4pm

MOUNT HERMAN SKI CENTRE

The summit of Mt Herman (2770m — 9088 ft) is actually in Syria
territory, but the lower southern slopes at the village of Neve At
are home to Israel's only ski resort, with the season lasting fro
late December to early April. Most of the ski-runs are for th
average to competent skier, with the longest being 2.5km. Ther
are separate chair-lifts for skiers and spectators. Skis, boots, stock
etc are available for hire. Prices are fairly high, unless you ar
staying at the Holiday Village in the town, ph 069-41744, whe
admission, lifts and lessons are included in the rates.

There are unreliable bus services to the slopes from Qiry
Shemona and Katzrin.

MAS'ADA

Back on Route 99 is the Druze village of Mas'ada, not to b
confused with Masada on the Dead Sea. The village is ver
picturesque, but the Druze here are very different from those i
other parts of the country. These are extremely anti-Israel, an
actively support Syria. They are very friendly to visitors, so thei
politics won't affect you. There is a good restaurant on the shore
of a small lake called Birket Ram (the High Lake).

KATZRIN

Katzrin is not a particularly attractive town, but some backpacker
use it as a base for touring the Golan, staying at the Golan-Katzri
Field Study Centre, ph 069-61 352. One important fact about th
town is that it has the only petrol station in the Golan.

GAMLA

Situated about 15km (9 miles) south of Katzrin, but not on a bus route, is what is thought to be the site of ancient Gamala. In the early stages of the Great Revolt (66–70AD) Gamala was under siege by the Romans. Josephus Flavius records in *The Jewish War* that the citizens refused to surrender, relying on the natural inaccessibility of the town and the additional fortifications that Josephus had had built. Josephus described the layout of the town — "Sloping down from a towering peak is a spur like a long shaggy neck, behind which rises a symmetrical hump, so that the outline resembles that of a camel; hence the name, the exact form of the word being obscured by the local pronunciation [*gamal* is Hebrew for camel]. On the face and both sides it is cut off by impassable ravines. Near the tail it is rather more accessible, where it is detached from the hill; but here too, by digging a trench across, the inhabitants made access very difficult. Built against the almost vertical flank the houses were piled on top of one another, and the town seemed to be hung in mid-air and on the point of tumbling on top of itself from its very steepness."

According to Josephus, the Jews put up a good fight when the Romans, under the leadership of Vespasian, finally attacked and for a time it looked as they might hold the town. But it ended the same way as Masada, with 5,000 Jewish men, women and children throwing themselves into the ravines, and two women escaping to tell Josephus all about it.

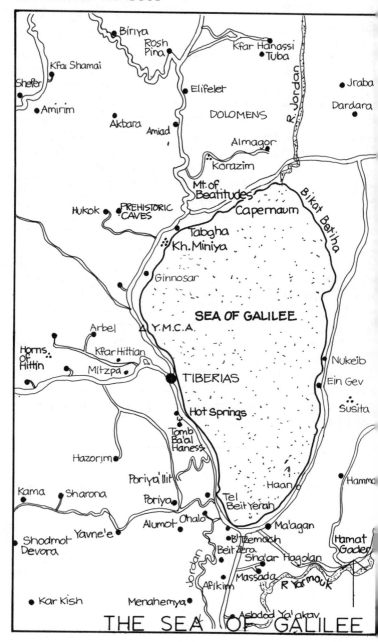

THE SEA OF GALILEE

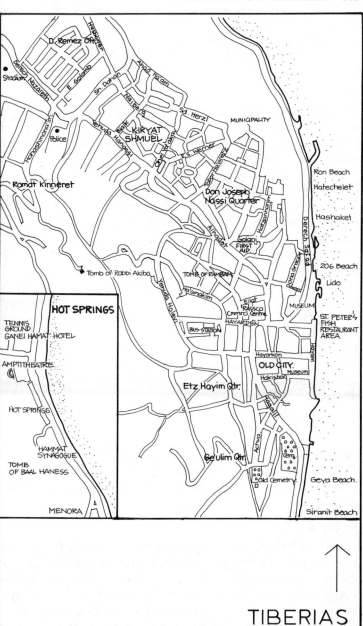

TIBERIAS

THE SEA OF GALILEE

The Sea of Galilee is actually a fresh-water lake, 22km (14 miles) long and 12km (8 miles) at its widest point, and it is often referred to as the dam of Israel. In fact when it formed part of the border with Syria, the Syrians had a plan to dry up the lake, and so dry up Israel. Fortunately it was never put into action.

The sea has had many name changes — the Old Testament refers to it as the Sea of Kinnereth, the Gospels of Matthew and Mark as the Sea of Galilee, John preferred the Sea of Tiberias, Mark played it safe in another part of his Gospel and wrote 'the Sea', and Luke, maybe more realistically, 'the Lake'. Josephus Flavius, who did not always get everything right, talks of the Lake of Gennesar, and the Israelis today call it the Kinneret. The shores of the sea have been inhabited since prehistoric times, confirmed by the finding, in 1925, of a male skull from the Palaeolithic period. The most important person who lived in the area was Jesus Christ, and it is around here that you will be actually walking in His footsteps.

There are many species of fish found in the Sea, and fishing is still an important industry. The St Peter fish, unique to these waters, is readily available in the restaurants.

TIBERIAS

Tiberias is situated on the south-western shore of the Sea of Galilee, and is in fact the only town on the shores. Its main industry is tourism, as it's the ideal base for touring the holy and historic sites.

HISTORY

Herod Antipas, the son of Herod the Great, and the Herod who executed John the Baptist, established a new city on the shores of the Sea of Galilee in 18AD, and named it after the Roman Emperor Tiberius. He had obviously inherited his father's flamboyant taste in buildings as the city had a gold-roofed palace, a stadium and a huge synagogue, but he made the mistake of building them on the site of the ancient cemetery of Rakat, which made the city unsuitable for Jewish settlement. But it was always hard to go against a Herod, and eventually the people unwillingly began to take up residence.

During the Jewish Revolt (66–70AD), Vespasian, the Roman general, was ready to fight to take the city but met with no resistance so the buildings remained unscathed. Tiberias was self-governing in the Roman period, minting its own coins, having its own calendar, and ruling over a large part of the surrounding territory. In the 2nd century AD, Rabbi Shimon Bar Yochai purified the city making it suitable for settlement, and the Jewish population increased, particularly after the failure of the Bar Kochba Revolt, when the Jews moved away from the Mediterranean coastal towns. By the 3rd century the city area was about 80ha (200 acres), and it became the capital of the Galilee, and the seat of the Jewish High Court. Sages and scholars came from far and near and the Mishnah and the Talmud were completed here, and the vowels were added to the Hebrew alphabet. All these achievements made Tiberias one of the country's four holy cities.

The Crusaders captured Tiberias in 1099, but lost it to Saladin in 1187 at the Horns of Hattin. The city then declined and was further destroyed by earthquakes.

In 1562, Tiberias was given to Don Joseph Nasi by Suleiman the Magnificent. Don Joseph tried to revive the city, but the results of his efforts are debatable.

In the 18th century, a Bedouin, Daher el-Omar tried to restore the city, and invited Turkish Jews to settle there. They were joined in 1777 by members of a Jewish sect from Eastern Europe. But in 1837 there was another massive earthquake and the town was partially destroyed.

Tiberias recovered very slowly, and has had its share of Arab riots. It was involved in the War of Independence in 1948. After the war it quadrupled its population with the numbers of Jewish refugees arriving in Israel. The population today is in the vicinty of 30,000.

HOW TO GET THERE

By Bus
There are regular service to Tiberias from Jerusalem, Tel Aviv, Safed, Nazareth, Beit She'an and Haifa. These buses do not run on Shabbat.

By Car
Tiberias is 157km (98 miles) from Jerusalem, 132km (82 miles) from Tel Aviv, 36km (22 miles) from Safed, 29km (18 miles) from Nazareth, 37km (23 miles) from Beit She'an and 69km (43 miles) from Haifa.

TOURIST INFORMATION
The Government Tourist Information Office is at 8 Alhadif Street, ph 720 992. Open Sun–Thurs 8am–6pm, Fri 8am–2pm.

ACCOMMODATION
As mentioned before, Tiberias is a tourist town, so there is no shortage of accommodation. The rates we quote here are for a double room, plus breakfast, per night, in US Dollars, and should be used as a guide only. The Telephone Area Code is 06.

5-star Hotels
Galei Kinnereth, 1 Kaplan Street, ph 792 331 — $145; Tiberias Plaza, Habanim Street, ph 792 233 — $145.

4-star Hotels
Jordan River, Habanim Street, ph 792 950 — $110; Ganei Hamat, Habanim Street (near Hot Springs), ph 792 890 — $90; Kinar, NE Sea of Galilee, ph 763 670 — $75; Ron Beach, Gdud Ba'ak Street, ph 791 350 — $72; Washington, 13 Zeidel Street, ph 791 861 — $68; Golan, 14 Achad Ha'am Street, ph 791 901 — $64; Ariston, 19 Herzel Boulevard, ph 790 244 — $64.

3-star Hotels
Quiet Beach, Gdud Ba'ak Road, ph 790 125 — $52–80; Peer, 2 Ohel Ya'acov, ph 791 641 — $55; Tiberias, 19 Ohel Ya'acov, ph 792 270 — $54; Galilee, Elhadef Street, ph 791 166 — $54; Astoria, 13 Ohei Ya'acov Street, ph 722 351 — $45; Daphna, POB 502, ph 792 261 — $45; Eden, 4 Nazareth Street, Kiryat Shmuei, ph 790 070 — $40.

2-star Hotels
Continental, 2 Alhadeff Street, ph 720 018 — $42; Arnon, 28 Hashomer Street, ph 720 181 — $40.

LOCAL TRANSPORT

In the town centre, it is possible to see everything on foot. To get to places around the Sea of Galilee, there are reasonable bus services along the western shore, and infrequent services along the eastern shore, but none around the north. If you haven't hired a car to get here, the best way to get around is to hire a bicycle, but keep in mind that the circumference of the Sea is 55km (34 miles), and it is advisable to start out early in the morning to beat the heat.

Also, most of the sites are 'holy' and require modest dress, so you'll need to take the extra clothes in a bag *with your water bottle.*

Bicycles can be hired from Easy Wave Rent-a-Bike, ph 20 123, or from the Nahum Hostel, ph 21 505.

EATING OUT

Along Hayarden Street, between Habanim Street and the bus station, are the best felafel shops.

There are several seafood restaurants specialising in the St Peter fish on the waterfront, but I'd recommend Fish On The Roof, ph 792 233, in the Tiberias Plaza. It is a bit more expensive, but remember the fish may be a 'once in a lifetime' experience.

The restaurant at the Hot Springs is excellent.

SIGHTSEEING

Old City
If you are expecting something like the old cities of Jerusalem or Akko, forget it. The earthquake of 1837 destroyed part of the city of Tiberias, and the survivors would naturally have taken stones from the walls to repair their own dwellings, so what can be seen now is part-Crusader, repaired in the 18th century and again in the early 19th century. There is also a castle, now housing a complex of studios and galleries, which is referred to as the Crusader Castle, but it was probably built much later in the 18th century.

Tombs of the Rabbis

In Yohanan Ben-Zakkai Street is the tomb of Tiberias' most famous resident, Rabbi Moshe Ben-Nahman. He was born in Spain in 1135, and is regarded as a great religious scholar and authority since the Talmudic period of the 4th century. He was also a philosopher, physician and scientist.

Near to the above tomb is that of Rabbi Yohanan Ben-Zakkai, a great sage, who during the Roman siege of Jerusalem, convinced the Roman general Vespasian to allow him to leave the city and settle on the coast, assuring the continuation of Jewish law and learning after Jerusalem was defeated.

Up the hill is the tomb of Rabbi Akiva, another great scholar. Born in 50AD, he was tortured to death in 135AD at Tiberias for his part in the Bar Kochba Revolt.

The tomb of Rabbi Meir Ba'al Hanes is a few kilometres away, behind Hammat Tiberias (hot springs). This rabbi from the 2nd century helped to compile the Mishnah. His tomb is one of the holiest places in Israel for Jews. He was a pupil of Rabbi Akiva, and was known as the 'Miracle-Maker'. Legend says that he took a vow never to lie down until the Messiah came, so he is buried in an upright position.

The tomb has two synagogues, one Sephardic and the other Ashkenazi, and there are special ceremonies conducted here for the Lag B'Omer holiday.

St Peter's Franciscan Church

Also known as Terra Sancta, St Peter's was built by the Crusaders in the 12th century. It subsequently became a mosque under Muslim control, a caravanserai when the Turks took over, and then reverted to a church. It was rebuilt in 1870, extended in 1903 and restored in 1944. It has a boat-shaped nave in keeping with Peter's original profession as a fisherman. The church is open daily 8–11.45am and 3–5.30pm.

Church and Monastery of the Apostles

A Greek Orthodox complex, built on the site of a Byzantine monastery, the church has four chapels — one dedicated to St Peter, one to Mary Magdalene, one to St Nicholas, and one to the Disciples.

Hot Springs

About 2km from the centre of the city is the site of the Biblical town of Hammath (Joshua 19:35) and it is here that the hot springs are found. They contain high amounts of sulphuric, muriatic and calcium salts, and are believed to be good for sufferers of rheumatism, arthritis, gout and nervous complaints. There are many legends surrounding the origins of the springs, but it is obvious that they are a natural phenomonen, and have probably been enjoyed by many since the Stone Age.

There are two complexes — Tiberias Hot Springs and Young Tiberias Hot Springs. The older of the two is for people with serious skin problems, while the more modern is open to the general public, and offers thermal pools and massages. Both are open Sun–Thurs 8am–8pm, Fri 8am–2.30pm, Sat 8.30am–8pm, and the prices are quite reasonable. If you don't feel up to the 2km walk, take Bus nos. 2 or 5 from the city.

Behind the springs there is a museum, the Ernest Lehman, which houses a reconstruction of the ancient town of Hammath, complete with the synagogue and mosaic floor. Open daily 8am– 5pm.

Sea of Galilee

To some Christians a trip on the Sea of Galilee is the highlight of a tour of Israel. After all, this is where Jesus walked on water (Matthew 14:22–33), calmed the tempest (Matthew 8:23–27) and told His disciples to cast their nets on the other side, when they couldn't catch any fish (John 21:4–8).

On a windless day it is hard to imagine a 'tempest' ever blowing up, but when the winds come from the west through the hills, the water becomes very rough and quite dangerous.

The Kinneret Sailing Company have a year round service from their wharf at the Tiberias Promenade to Kibbutz Ein Gev and return. In summer there are as many as 4 sailings in each direction per day. They can also arrange charter trips for groups between Capernaum and Ein Gev. For more information, ph 721 831, or call into their office on the Promenade.

Incidentally, do not expect to see many fishermen on these cruises as most of the fishing in the Sea of Galilee is done at night.

Beaches

All of the beaches in the vicinity of Tiberias have an entrance fee, but as they are well kept, it doesn't seem much to ask. Blue Beach and Shell Beach have canoe hire; Blue Beach and Quiet Beach have swimming pools, and Lido Kinneret has water-skiing equipment available.

TOURS
There are free walking tours leaving from the Tiberias Plaza Hotel at 10am, twice a week December–March, three times a week April–November. Phone 792 233 for further information. There is another on Sundays, also starting at 10am, but leaving from the Galei Kinneret Hotel, ph 792 331.

Galilee Tours have tours beginning in Tiberias, and their local office is at 10 Jordan Street, ph 720 330. Tour 443 is a full-day trip to the Gollan Heights, departing at 9am on Tuesday, for US$22 per person. Tour 463 is a two-day tour to Golan, Safed and Acre, departing at 9am on Tuesday, for US$115 per person. Egged Tours at the Central Bus Station, ph 720 474, have a tour of the Sea of Galilee leaving every four hours from the Bus Station, Sun–Fri 8.30am–4.30pm. It is an explorer-type tour where you can get off and stay at any place, and pick up the next bus.

CIRCLE AROUND THE SEA OF GALILEE

MIGDAL

Following the road that circles the Sea, roughly 4km north of Tiberius on the right hand side, you come to a white-domed building and some ruins. This is the site of the village of Magdala, where Mary Magdalene lived. In actual fact she should be called Mary the Magdalene, and this is not the only way she has been misrepresented. She is regarded by most as a women of somewhat tarnished reputation, but in fact the only mention of her life previous to ministering to Christ is in Luke 8:2 "Mary called Magdalene, out of whom had come seven demons", which could mean some type of sickness.

Magdala means 'tower' in Arabic and the old fishing village was named for its defence tower. Further up the road, approximately 2km, is the modern Jewish village of Migdal, which is Hebrew for 'tower'.

Behind Migdal is a canyon, Wadi Hamam, which the Druze believe contains the tomb of the Prophet Jethro (Moses' father-in-law) whom they revere, and this is their most important shrine.

A few kilometres past Migdal is Nof Ginossar, and the Kibbutz Ginnosar. In the lake bed near the Kibbutz a fishing boat of the Second Temple Period was uncovered. It seems that Israel experienced several dry winters, lowering the level of the Sea and revealing the boat lodged in the sand. Archaeologists were quick to retrieve the boat and have gone to great lengths to preserve it. They intend to build a museum to house it, but at present it is in a shed behind the regional museum of Bet Allon.

TABGHA

Tabgha was known by the Greeks as Heptapegon, Seven Springs, and is the valley east of the road about 12km (7 miles) north of Tiberias. Buses 459, 941 and 963 from Tiberius travel to this area.

Gloriously peaceful, and thankfully not commercialised, it all seems just·the right setting for the events that occurred around here — the Loaves and Fishes miracle, the Sermon on the Mount and the appearance of Christ after His resurrection.

Church of the Multiplication of the Loaves and Fishes
Believed to be the site of the miracle where Jesus fed about 5000 men, plus women and children, with five loaves and two fish. "So they all ate and were filled, and they took up twelve baskets full of the fragments that remained." (Matthew 14:20).

The German Benedictine church standing here today has been built on the site of a 5th century Byzantine church, whose beautiful mosaic floor is still preserved. The design is mostly of flora and fauna of the area, but Egyptian influence is recognised with the incorporation of lotus flowers and a Nilometer. Underneath this floor there are parts of a 4th century church.

There is a simple but striking mosaic in front of the altar with two fish and a basket of loaves.

The church is open daily 7.30am–6pm April–September, 8am–5pm October-March.

Church of the Primacy of St Peter
The church was built by the Franciscans in 1933 on the site of a 4th century church, and parts of the old walls are still visible. In front

of the altar is a flat rock, known as Mensa Christi (Christ's Table). It is believed that here Christ and His disciples (after his Resurrection) ate breakfast and Christ told Peter to "Feed my lambs." (John 21:15)

Near the waters of the sea, in front of the church, steps have been cut into the rock, and some believe that this is where Christ appeared to the disciples, but it seems more likely that they come from a later period.

Church of the Mount of the Beatitudes
Situated on a hill across from the Heptapegon is the Franciscan Church of the Beatitudes. It is built on the site of a 4th century church, and the money for the present building actually came from the Italian dictator Mussolini in 1937, to celebrate an anniversary of his regime, but the nuns who look after the church will tell you the money came from the Vatican.

The church is octagonal symbolising the eight Beatitudes (Matthew 5:1–10), and has eight small stained glass windows each inscribed with one. Around the altar there are symbols of the seven virtues. From the verandah around the church are some of the best views of the Sea of Galilee.

The church is open daily 8am–noon, 2.30–5pm.

CAPERNAUM

Capernaum, where Christ began his ministry, is located about 3km east of Tabgha, and its a pleasant walk, if you have remembered to bring water. The building that stands out is the Greek Orthodox Monastery, which actually looks better at a distance than close up. But that is not of much interest, and they don't encourage visitors. The main attraction of Capernaum is the open air archaeological museum of the Franciscans.

The New Testament has many references to Christ in Capernaum. Matthew 4:13–17 and Mark 2:1 state that Christ lived there; Mark 1:21 tells of Christ teaching in the local synagogue. There were also miracles performed in Capernaum: casting out an evil spirit (Mark 1:23–28); curing Peter's mother-in-law (Mark 1:30–31); healing the centurion's servant (Luke 7:1–10) to name a few.

Despite all this, the people suspected Him and refused to follow His preachings, causing Him to say, "And you, Capernaum, who are exalted to heaven, will be brought down to Hades" (Matthew 11:23).

Just past the entrance to the museum is a wall of decorated stones from a syngague dated around the 2nd or 3rd century. Then you come to some excavations of houses, one of which is believed to be the house Péter lived in. To the left there are the remains of a late 4th century synagogue, which the sign says was built on the Synagogue of Jesus, then to the left of the synagogue, surrounded by a wire fence, are stones which, it is believed, are part of the synagogue where Jesus preached.

To the right of the excavated houses is a building under construction, which looks like a space station, but will probably be a church of some kind, but whatever is planned for it, it seems to be completely out of character with the area.

The museum is open daily 8.30am–4.15pm, and the people in charge are extremely strict about modest clothing. Outside the complex there is a snack bar and toilets.

THE EASTERN SHORE

Leaving Capernaum, continuing on the sea road, it is about 4km to the Jordan River crossing, then roughly 2km further on a road branches off to the left to the northern Golan and Mount Hermon. At the next intersection, take the turn to the right for the road leading south along the eastern shore of the Sea.

A short distance along there is another side road to the left to *Gamla* (see previous chapter), and the next settlement is *Ramot*, a popular holiday spot with the Israelis. Near the next turn off to the left is the historical site of Kursi.

The Byzantines during the 5th and 6th centuries believed that *Kursi* was the place mentioned in Luke 8:26–30 where Jesus exorcised the devils from a Gadarene (or Gerasene) man, and the devils entered a herd of swine grazing hearby. Consequently Kursi became a prosperous monastery with hospices for the many pilgrims to the Sea of Galilee, and a partially restored church indicates the level of workmanship of this period.

5km (three miles) south of Kursi, is *Kibbutz Ein-Gev*. The

Kibbutz is not only built on a prehistoric site, it has become popular as a lunch-stop because of the excellent seafood restaurant, supplied by its own fishing industry. It also has good holiday facilities. There is a scheduled ferry service to Tiberias across the Sea, and a charter service to Capernaum. It is here that the prestigious Ein Gev Spring Festival of music and dance is held every year.

It is worth taking a detour at the next turn to the left, about 10km (6 miles) from Ein-Gev. This road leads to *Hammat Gader* on the Jordanian Border. Before you reach the complex the smell will tell you there are sulphur springs ahead. The Hammat Gader complex is in green parkland, and has Roman ruins and a crocodile park. The hot springs here are much cheaper than the indoor baths at Tiberias.

The Roman baths of Hammat Gader are supposed to have been surpassed only by those at Naples. They were built in the 2nd century AD, and actually enhanced by an earthquake in 363 which increased their size. The site continued to be used until the early 10th century, and archaeologists have been working since 1979 confirming many early historical references to the springs. Originally there were several pools of different temperatures, the smallest was apparently reserved for lepers, and the hottest spring (51C) was known as Ma'ayan HaGehinom (Hell's Pool).

The complex is open Sat–Thurs 8am–4pm, Fri 8am–3pm, and there is a bus service from the Tiberias bus station.

Back on the Sea road the next settlement is *Deganya*, the oldest kibbutz in Israel, founded in 1909. It is on the eastern bank of the Jordan River, and on the western bank is another kibbutz, Kinneret, founded in 1911.

The New Testament tells that Jesus was baptised by John the Baptist in the Jordan River (Matthew 3:13–17) and a baptism site has been built at the entrance to Kibbutz Kinneret, but it must be pointed out that this is NOT where Jesus was baptised. The traditional site of His baptism is in Jordan and not accessible to visitors.

The last town before reaching Tiberias on the shore road is *Hammath*. It was destroyed and rebuilt many times, but was a lively Jewish town until the 8th century. The most interesting sight here is the old synagogue, which has a beautiful mosaic floor rom the 4th century, not dissimilar from the one at Bet Alfa (see ollowing chapter).

Church of the Annunciation, Nazareth.

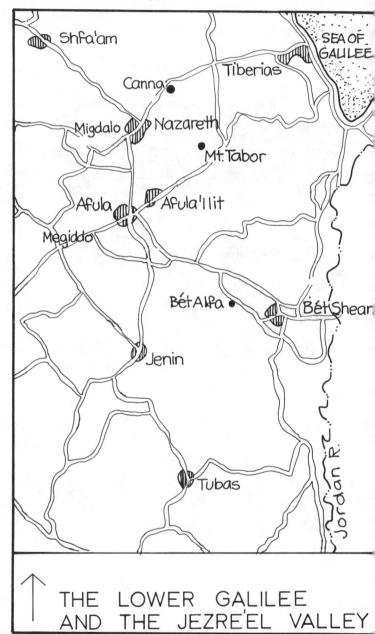

THE LOWER GALILEE
AND THE JEZRE'EL VALLEY

THE LOWER GALILEE AND THE JEZRE'EL VALLEY

The Lower Galilee is famous as the area in which Our Lady and St Joseph lived before the birth of Christ and during His boyhood, and here also is Mount Tabor, believed to be the mountain of the Transfiguration.

The Jezre'el Valley is roughly triangular in shape, with its points at Bet Shearim in the north-west, Mount Tabor in the north-east and Jenin in the south. It is now a rich agricultural district, but was a mixture of swampland and rocky terrain before the influx of migration early this century.

The Jezre'el Valley is linked to the Bet She'an Valley by the narrow Harod Valley, and south of Bet She'an the land becomes semi-desert. In every period of history, these valleys have been crossed by major arterial roads. The Via Maris, which ran from Egypt to Mesopotamia split into three after leaving the coast. Where each route reached the Jezre'el Valley, a city was built to guard the pass, the most famous of these being Megiddo.

NAZARETH

Once an insignificant village, Nazareth is now quite a large town with a predominantly Arab population. Nazareth Illit, in Upper Nazareth, is a quite separate Jewish town. Consequently, in old Nazareth the Sabbath is celebrated on a Sunday, and many of the shops are closed. The town is also subject to many strikes, due to PLO influence, when most places are closed, so it is wise to check with tourist authorities before setting out. The strikes are apparently advertised, as when I was there everybody knew the day before that Nazareth would be closed the next day. Women travelling on their own should be particularly careful in this town, as the local Arabs still look on foreign women as fair game.

HISTORY
The Gospel of St Luke tells, "the angel Gabriel was sent by God to a city of Galilee named Nazareth to a virgin betrothed to a man

whose name was Joseph, of the house of David. The virgin's name was Mary." (1:26–27) So Christians believe that this town was the home of Mary and Joseph before the birth of Christ, and after the Holy Family returned from Egypt "they returned to Galilee, to their own city, Nazareth" (Luke 2:39).

It seems that Nazareth had a Christian community until about the 3rd century, then there is not much known until the 5th century when the Byzantines built a church on the site of the Annunciation. The Crusaders made Nazareth their capital of the Galilee in the 12th century, and rebuilt the Byzantine church, and also erected another dedicated to the angel Gabriel, but these were destroyed by the Mamelukes in the 13th century.

The Franciscans bought the ruins of the Church of the Annunciation in 1620, cleared the site and built a new one in 1730, which in turn was demolished and the present church erected in 1955.

HOW TO GET THERE
By Bus
There are services every hour from Afulla, Tiberius, Akko and Haifa. The service from Jerusalem operates twice a day, and there is also one from Tel Aviv, which is more frequent.

By Car
Nazareth is 45km (28 miles) from Akko, 35km (22 miles) from Haifa, 157km (98 miles) from Jerusalem, 102km (63 miles) from Tel Aviv and 29km (18 miles) from Tiberias.

TOURIST INFORMATION
The Israel Government Tourist Office is in Casa Nova Street, ph 573 003, and is open Mon–Fri 8am–5pm, Sat 8am–3pm, closed Sunday and Christian Holidays.

ACCOMMODATION
There are quite a few hospices and a youth hostel, but only three hotels, all rated 3-star. The prices listed are for a double room, plus breakfast, per night in US Dollars. The Telephone Area Code is 06.

Nazareth, ph 577 777 — $44; Grand New, St Joseph Street, ph 573 325 — $41; Hagalil, Paulus VI Street, ph 571 311.

LOCAL TRANSPORT

There is no need for any transport. Most of the sights and hotels are within walking distance of each other.

EATING OUT

The hotels have dining rooms, bars and coffee shops, and Paulus VI and Casa Nova Streets have many restaurants and felafel stands. The restaurants serve mostly Middle-Eastern food, but the hotels and hospices generally have European fare.

SIGHTSEEING

Basilica of the Annunciation

Although some might argue that the building is too modern-looking, everyone has to agree that it is clean and well looked after — a nice change from most of the other important Christian sites.

Inside the courtyard to the right of the entrance there are many mosaic panels on the wall, all with an Annunciation theme, which are gifts from countries all over the world. Some are very ornate, whilst others are simple, but they are all thought-provoking.

The bronze doors of the main entrance to the church are works of art in themselves, depicting the major events in the life of Christ, and other Biblical figures. Inside there are actually two churches. The lower is built over what is believed to be Mary's house, therefore the place of the Annunciation. Here there are remains of the Byzantine and Crusader churches.

The spiral stairs near the entrance lead to the upper church. It is over 60m long and 25m wide, and the dome is about 60m above the crypt. The beautiful stained-glass windows throw brilliant colours on the bare stone. All around the walls are banners, actually wall-panels, also gifts from Catholic communities of different nations. Most have madonna and child themes, but not all, for example Canada's shows Mary amongst the lakes and forests of Canada, and America's is Mary as described in Revelations. Personally, I was a bit disappointed with the one from my own country, Australia, but that's life.

The Basilica is open daily April–September 8.30–11.45am and 2–5pm, October–March 9–11.45am and 2–4.30pm, Sun 2–5pm.

Outside the Basilica, to the left, is a bapistry which was built over the remains of a Jewish mikveh (ritual bath) from a synagogue.

St Joseph's Church

Up the steps near the bapistry and past the Terra Sancta College is the Church of St Joseph, which is believed to be built on the site of his carpentry workshop, or some even say his house. Excavations have shown that neither may be the case as there is evidence of a mikveh (ritual bath) of the same period, indicating that this may have been a synagogue. It really doesn't matter much, if it was his workshop well and good, if it was a synagogue it would have been the one he attended, so nothing is really lost.

Market

The market in Casa Nova Street is mainly for the locals, but further along the street, and in Paulus XI Street are the tourist shops, which specialise in eastern-style dresses and religious trinkets. In the market is the 'synagogue', which is not a synagogue at all, as it is owned by Greek Catholics. The building is very old though, and is believed to be built on the site of the synagogue mentioned in Luke 4:16–30, where Jesus went on the Sabbath and was given the book of Isaiah to read to the congregation.

The Church of the Boy Jesus

The church was built in 1918 by the French Salesian Order, and is considered by some to be the finest church in the town. It's quite a walk up the hill to the church and school next door, but the view of the surrounding countryside makes it worth the effort.

St Gabriel's Church and Mary's Well

This is another case of one set of people believing the generally accepted place is incorrect, as in Christ's Tomb in Jerusalem. Some people believe that the angel Gabriel appeared to Mary when she was at a well, not at the grotto in the basilica. This particular Greek Orthodox church was built in the late 17th century, but there had been churches on this site previously, one from the Crusader period and probably one before. The well is supplied by a natural spring, which is pretty insignificant now, and I find it hard to believe that the present well is the original.

OUTLYING ATTRACTIONS

CANA

Everybody remembers the wedding at Cana where Christ turned water into wine, because I suppose we would all like to have a guest with such powers, but not many realise that Cana was the venue of another miracle. A nobleman went up to Jesus when He again visited Cana, and asked Him to go to Capernaum to cure his son, and He replied, "Unless you people see signs and wonders you will by no means believe...... Go your way; your son lives." (John 4:46–54). John also tells us that the disciple Nathanael came from Cana (21:2).

Cana is ten minute's drive from Nazareth on the road to Tiberias, and buses leave from near Mary's Well.

As in other places, there are two religions who believe their churches have been built on the site of the miracle — the Franciscan's and the Greek Orthodox.

The Franciscan Church was built in 1881, and is easily spotted because of its white towers. Near the church, which has remnants of a mosaic pavement beneath the floor, is the St Nathanael Chapel, purported to be built on the site of his house.

The Greek Orthodox church has some ancient stone vessels which some believe were actually used at the wedding.

THE HORNS OF HATTIN

Travelling on the same road a further 14km (9 miles) brings into sight the Horns of Hattin, the twin-peaked hill where Saladin and his Moslems defeated the Crusaders on July 4, 1187, thereby gaining control of most of the country.

MOUNT TABOR

Mount Tabor (588m — 1911 ft) is south-east of Nazareth, but is reached by taking Route 75 south to Afula, then the turn-off to the north on Route 65. There is a bus service, but it stops at the foot of the mountain.

It was at the foot of Mt Tabor that the prophetess/judge Deborah and her general, Barak, routed the Canaanite army and sang her victory song (Judges 4–5). And opposite Mount Tabor is the modern kibbutz of Ein Dor, built on the site of the ancient En

Dor where Saul consulted a medium to get in touch with the dead Samuel on the eve of his battle with the Phillistines (1 Samuel 28:7–19).

Christian tradition nominates Mount Tabor as the place where Jesus took Peter, James and John his brother "and was transfigured before them. His face shone like the sun, and his clothes became as white as the light. And behold, Moses and Elijah appeared to them, talking with him" (Matthew 17:2–3). Peter then suggested that they make three 'arbours', one for Jesus, one for Moses and one for Elijah, and churches built on the site have generally had three chapels, as does the present Franciscan Church of the Transfiguration.

The church is open April–September Mon–Sat 8.30–11.45am, 2–5.45pm, Sunday and holy days 2–5.45pm. October–March Mon–Sat 9–11.45am, 2–4.45pm Sunday and holy days 2–4.45pm

The view from the top of the mountain is stunning.

BET SHEARIM

Bet Shearim is only about 19km (12 miles) from Haifa, and can be reached by bus from there, but it is actually part of the Galilee hill country.

It was an important Jewish town, the seat of the Sanhedrin during the 2nd century, and the home of Rabbi Yehuda Hanassi who compiled the Mishnah. When the area around Jerusalem was closed to Jews, stopping them from burying their dead on the Mount of Olives, Bet Shearim became the logical burying ground because of the holy work of Rabbi Hanassi. It was thus used for over 100 years.

In the 1930s excavations of the town began. Tombs and catacombs were discovered, but over the years all had been looted and anything of monetary value removed. There is a wealth of information for archaeologists in the motifs and inscriptions on the sarcophagi.

Unless you are into this sort of stuff, I wouldn't go out of my way to visit here, but you will find what is left of a 2nd century synagogue, a 4th century olive press and a 2nd century basilica

MEGIDDO

In historical records Megiddo is first mentioned as the site of the attack by the Egyptian pharaoh Tutmoses III in 1468BC. Excavations have revealed that it existed as early as the fourth millenium, having uncovered 26 different layers of habitation, the last dated at about the 4th century BC.

The Egyptians, after Tutmoses' victory, retained control of the city for probably one hundred years, and then it must have passed to the Canaanites, for Judges 1:27 tells that the children of Israel did not drive out "the inhabitants of Megiddo and its villages; for the Canaanites were determined to dwell in that land".

In the time of Solomon (10th century BC) it became, along with Hazor and Gezer, one of the "chariot cities" (1 Kings 9:15) and therefore important for defence purposes. Excavations have revealed many chariot stables which were originally thought to be those of Solomon, but have since been accredited to King Ahab, who was known to have a chariot army in the 9th century.

During the Roman period Megiddo became part of the Via Maris (Way of the Sea), the highway linking Egypt and Mesopotamia.

For some unknown reason the city became uninhabited by the 4th century BC, but it's importance as a battlefield came to the fore again in World War I, and during the 1948 War of Independence. Incidentally, when General Allenby was granted a peerage he took the title Lord Allenby of Meggido.

Meggido is better known today as Armageddon, taken from the Hebrew Har Megiddo which means Mount of Meggido, the place mentioned by St John in Revelation as the final battlefield.

HOW TO GET THERE

By Bus
The bus service from Nazareth to Hadera has a stop about 10 minutes' walk from the site.

By Car
Megiddo is near the intersection of Routes 66 and 65. It is approximately 22km (14 Miles) from Nazareth.

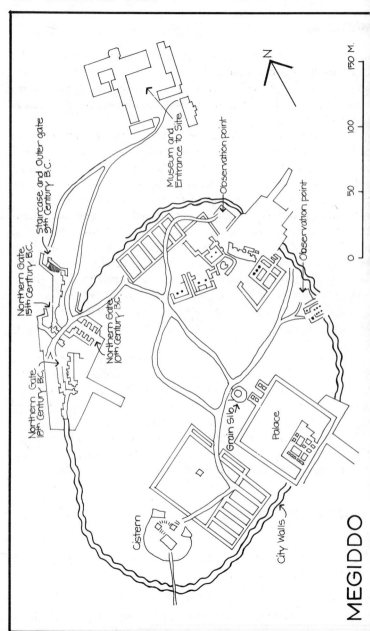

N

0   50   100   150 M.

Staircase and Outer gate
9th Century B.C.

Museum and
Entrance to Site

Observation point

Observation point

Northern Gate
15th Century B.C.

Northern Gate
16th Century B.C.

Northern Gate
10th Century B.C.

Grain Silo

Cistern

Palace

City walls

MEGIDDO

SIGHTSEEING

Near the entrance to the site is a small museum, in a building that was formerly the headquarters of the Rockefeller archaeological expedition. The museum has a snack bar and cafe. Behind is a roadway from the time of David which constituted the approach to the city. On top of the roadway was one from Solomon's time, and part of Solomon's massive gate can still be seen. It is flanked by towers, and the road within the gate has a triple guardroom on each side.

Other buildings of interest are those near the south edge of the tel surrounded by a wall, which are thought to be the home of the governor; and the two groups of stables belonging to King Ahab. In the middle of the tel is a large silo of the 8th century BC with two interior staircases, and at the eastern end, three Canaanite temples from 2000BC.

The *piece de resistance*, however, is the water-system, probably dating from the 9th century BC. It consists of a large shaft cut into the rock to a depth of 36.5m (120 ft) and then connected with a spring outside the city. The spring was well camouflaged by an earthern wall.

The site is open Sat–Thurs 8am–5pm, Fri 8am–4pm, and there is an admission fee.

EIN HAROD

From Megiddo, Route 65 leads to Afula, which has nothing to offer the visitor, and the intersection of Route 71, the Bet She'an road. About 15km (9 miles) along Route 71 is a turn-off to the right to the village of Gidona and the Spring of Harod. It was at this spring that Gideon gathered the Israelites for battle against the Midianites, and God told him to choose only 300, from the 22000 available, so that they would all know that it was His divine help that won the battle (Judges 7).

BET ALFA

Further along Route 71, at the white-washed prison, there is a turn-off to the right which leads to Kibbutz Heftziba, in which is the Bet Alfa synagogue. (There is sometimes confusion here as

Kibbutz Bet Alfa is the next settlement, but the synagogue is in Kibbutz Heftziba.)

In 1928, when the workers were getting the Kibbutz established, they were digging an irrigation channel and uncovered one of the best-preserved mosaic floors in Israel, that of a synagogue of the 6th century AD, with an inscription dedicating it in the reign of Justinian. Another inscription tells that the work was done by Marianos and his son, Aninas.

The floor is divided into three panels. The upper one is no surprise for it has all the Jewish symbols common in synagogues of this time, the Ark, a menorah, the ram's horn, lion, etc. The middle panel is the one that seems out of place for it has the Hellenistic wheel of the Zodiac with the figures labelled in Hebrew, and the sun-god Helios driving his chariot in the centre. If you look closely, though, you will note that the star signs are running anti-clockwise, which is a bit unusual. There are also depictions of the four seasons at each corner, depicted by human figures. The lowest panel shows the near-sacrifice of Isaac by his father Abraham (Genesis 22:1–19).

The site is open Sat–Thurs 8am–5pm, Fri 8am–4pm.

MOUNT GILBOA

Bet Alfa is actually at the foot of Mount Gilboa, the mountain where Saul and his three sons were killed by the Phillistines, and Saul's body was "fastened" to the wall of Beth Shan (1 Samuel 31:8–10). When David found out what had happened to Saul and his sons he cursed the mountain, saying "O mountains of Gilboa, let there be no dew, nor let there be rain upon you" (2 Samuel 1:21). This curse proved to be very effective resulting in a very brown mountain, that is until the modern Israelis stepped in with irrigation and plastic sheeting to make half the mountain extremely green. The contrast is very interesting.

SACHNE

About a kilometre south-east of Bet Alfa, on the bus route, is what could be described as an oasis, with landscaped grassland, plenty of trees and natural swimming pools connected by waterfalls. The temperature of the water is a steady 28C (82F), coming from a spring, and 'sachne' is Arabic for 'warm'. There are changing rooms, a snack bar and cafe, and facilities for picnicking. In the shallows of the pools there are tiny fish which tend to nibble your toes, but there don't seem to be any big brothers or sisters in the deeper water.

The park is known in Hebrew as Gan HaShlosha (Garden of the Three) commemorating three Jews that were killed here by Arabs in 1938.

The park is open Sat–Thurs 8am–5.30pm, Fri 8am–4.30pm, and there is an admission fee.

BET SHE'AN

Bet She'an is at the junction of two valleys, the Jezre'el and the Jordan, and so occupied a very stragic position in ancient times. The tel of the old city is in the northern part of the small town today, and although the size of the place has changed, Bet She'an has been occupied continuously for over 5000 years. Excavations have revealed that it was an Egyptian provincial capital in the 14th–12th centuries BC.

The Bible, in Judges 1:27, reveals that the tribe of Manasseh inherited Beth Shean, but lost it to the Philistines on Mount Gilboa, and Saul's body was hung on the city walls (1 Samuel 31).

In the 3rd century BC it was known as Scythopolis, and later it was the Roman capital of the Decapolis, a league of ten cities.

The most impressive sight for visitors today is the Roman theatre, built about 200AD, which, it is estimated (the upper tiers have not survived the ravages of time), held 8000 people. Open Sat–Thurs 8am–5pm, Fri 8am–4pm. There is an admission fee.

A few hundred metres north of the bus station on the Tiberias road, there is a museum which was originally a Byzantine church, then a mosque, then a Turkish inn. The people in charge of the museum are very helpful, and will often point out things of interest off the beaten track. The museum is open Sun–Thurs 8.30am–3.30pm, Fri 8.30am–12.30pm. An admission fee is charged.

Bet She'an is on the Tiberias-Jerusalem bus route, and also has services to and from Afulla.

BELVOIR

Belvoir was a Crusader castle in the 12th century, and while it was not the biggest, it was one of the strongest, and probably had the most scenic surroundings, looking out over the Jesre'el and Jordan valleys. Sometimes it is possible to see the Sea of Galilee in the distance, and in fact, Belvoir means 'beautiful view'.

The Knights of St John completed this fortress in 1173, and managed to hold out against two attacks by Saladin in 1182–3. The Crusader armies were defeated by the Muslims in the Horns of Hattin in July 1187, and from then until January 1191 the Muslims tried to breach the defences of Belvoir. Finally the Crusaders were forced to surrender, but in a tribute to their bravery, Saladin allowed them to retreat to Tyre, with banners flying. Saladin and his men did not destroy the castle, but the Sultan of Damascus did in the early 13th century, having heard a rumour that the Crusaders were returning.

Today it is a toss-up as to which is the more impressive — the castle ruins or the view.

Unfortunately the local bus stop is about 6km from the castle, so if you decide to walk, make sure you have plenty of water.

The site is open Sat–Thurs 8am–5pm, Fri 8am–4pm, and there is an admission fee.